AN AMERICAN AMNESIA

AN AMERICAN AMNESIA

Bruce
Herschensohn

HOW THE

U.S. CONGRESS

FORCED

THE SURRENDERS

OF SOUTH VIETNAM

AND CAMBODIA

BEAUFORT BOOKS
New York

Library of Congress Cataloging-in-Publication Data

Herschensohn, Bruce, 1932-
  An American amnesia : how the U.S. Congress forced the surrenders
of South Vietnam and Cambodia / Bruce Herschensohn.
    p. cm.
  Includes bibliographical references.

  ISBN 978-0-8253-0632-7 (alk. paper)
  1. Vietnam War, 1961-1975—Peace. 2. United States—Politics and
government—1974-1977. 3. Vietnam—History—1975- 4. Cambodia—
History--1975-1979. 5. United States. Congress (94th, 1st session :
1975) 6. United States. Congress (94th, 2nd session : 1976) I. Title.
  DS559.7.H47 2010
  959.704'32--dc22

                                              2009046956

For inquiries about volume orders, please contact:

Beaufort Books
27 West 20th Street, Suite 1102
New York, NY 10011
sales@beaufortbooks.com

Published in the United States by Beaufort Books
www.beaufortbooks.com

Distributed by Midpoint Trade Books
www.midpointtrade.com

Printed in the United States of America

CONTENTS

AUTHOR'S NOTES

FOR EASE IN reading, those comments that are usually reserved for footnotes have instead been enclosed in brackets within the text itself. In that way, those details can either be easily read or skipped at the will of the individual reader.

Whereas the names of public figures are used, some names of non-public figures have been changed for their privacy. The names of most U.S. Foreign Service Officers, whose public versus private status are often debated, are not used.

When no attribution is given to conversations, those conversations took place in the presence of the author. Since they were not recorded or written concurrent with those conversations, they are often paraphrased, but they are as authentic as possible from notes taken shortly thereafter.

Any and all material designated as classified at the time has since been declassified.

INTRODUCTION

LIKE ALL TIMES, the 1960s and the 1970s will someday be so long ago that the world will be vacant of anyone who lived through them. Now, however, those decades are not so distant, and under ordinary conditions the years ahead would provide more than sufficient time to record the truth of those years. No rush; there would be plenty of opportunity to do that. But the conditions are not ordinary, as already there has developed a self-induced American amnesia so deep and so widespread that many in the new generation are being educated by teachers who inject their students with a hypodermic filled with fiction.

The serum contains ingredients that convince the student that during the war in which the United States fought in Southeast Asia, five U.S. Presidents were not as smart as their professor. The injection is painless; just a little pressure is felt at the time of the fluid's introduction. But after a while the fluid hardens in the student's system and it flourishes into delusions of how foreign policy should be enacted in the future.

It has already happened.

To be both brief and precise, this book came about because once a week during the fall semesters in the School of Public Policy at Pepperdine University there is an evening Foreign Policy Roundtable for those students who elect to attend. Generally, one session each semester is devoted to the subject of the Southeast Asian War that divided the people of the United States, and continues its profound effect on U.S. foreign affairs. Since the students are post-graduates, most often they have already studied that war in the colleges they previously attended. As the session goes on, something happens that at first was unexpected and now is very much expected: it is revealed that large gaps have been left in their education regarding the lives and deaths of Americans, Vietnamese, Laotians, and Cambodians during that period and beyond. Some students are justifiably confused.

A common dialogue has become: "How come I was never told these things at the college I attended?"

The only accurate answer has been, "I can only guess. It is my belief that the professor who taught you about that war didn't know, or *did* know and didn't want *you* to know."

This book is meant to fill in vacancies left in too many histories of the Southeast Asian War. Much of the information used is taken from notes, commentaries, speeches, articles, and other writings of mine during the 1960s and 1970s as those events were being lived.

It should be apparent by this book's short length regarding a long war that it is not meant to be a complete history of the war. Rather, it is meant to act as a supplement to history by recording those pertinent pieces of the past that have been tossed aside, successfully destroying so much of the truth and creating the book's title: *An American Amnesia.*

1

WHY WE FORGET

IT WAS A glorious morning at the White House. The best.
  "We Won!"
  "It's over!"
  "It's everything we fought for!"
  "It's V-V Day! Victory in Vietnam!"

Those were the words that could be heard coming from offices
of the West Wing and the Old Executive Office Building in the
White House Compound as office doors were opened so anyone in other offices or walking in those hallways could hear the
news. And then the office-holders went into the hallways and
there were cheers and tears of glee and there were embraces.

It was Tuesday, January the 23rd of 1973. After nearly
fourteen years of military involvement in Vietnam [since

President Eisenhower first sent U.S. military advisors to South Vietnam in April of 1959], the United States won its major objectives in an agreement signed by North Vietnam and the Viet Cong, as well as the United States and South Vietnam. But on the day you are reading this, very few Americans remember that victory and what happened to extinguish it two and one-quarter years after the signatures were penned beneath its promises.

Back on that January morning in 1973, Richard A. Moore, Special Counsel to the President, was standing in the narrow West Wing basement hallway by the White House Mess with a big smile on his old and glowing Irish face beneath his short butch-cut gray hair. He started groping around his pockets in his suit jacket that hung on his large frame. He was searching for something. He found it. He nodded to himself and reached in his inside jacket pocket for a small tin case with the name of Davidoff on its painted label. He opened its cover and took out one of the cigarette-sized cigars, put the case back in his pocket, and set the mini-cigar between his lips.

"Hey, Dick!" a Nixon aide said before walking into the Mess.

Richard A. Moore took the yet unlit mini-cigar from his lips and said, "Matt! What a day! What a day! You did it, Matt!"

Mathew Kinnard had absolutely nothing to do with it. "Dick, you know I didn't do it. *You* did it! *Congratulations*, Dick!"

"Now, Matt, you can just go on believing that if you want to. In fact, you can spread the word—but we both know who *really* did it. And it wasn't me and—I'm sorry, you're right—it wasn't you."

"It was the President."

"Nixon's the One!" He recited the old campaign slogan, almost swaying to it as if it was the opening bar of a song. "And what a way to begin the second term!"

"The President is going to speak tonight. Ray Price is the only one who isn't celebrating. He doesn't have time. He's locked in his office working on the 'nteenth draft of the speech. He's been up all night going back and forth to the President."

"Isn't it something? You know, in one day we win the war and Susan—you know, Clawson's secretary, Susan—Susan runs into me in the E.O.B. [Old Executive Office Building] in the Xerox Room, and she puts her arms around me and gives me a kiss! She was so happy she had tears in her eyes. But what man could ask for anything more in one day than victory in Vietnam and a kiss from Susan—I mean, both in the same day! On the cheek, of course. Nothing more. But for an old duffer like me, that's all I can possibly take in one day! And a smoke, of course." And he finally lit his mini-cigar.

It was called a cease-fire, but it was a great deal more than a cease-fire. The agreement made in Paris between the warring parties stated that "the Government of the United States of America and the Government of the Democratic Republic of Vietnam [North Vietnam] undertake to respect the following principles for the exercise of the South Vietnamese people's right to self-determination: (a) The South Vietnamese people's right to self-determination is sacred, inalienable and shall be respected by all countries. (b) The South Vietnamese people shall decide themselves the political future of South Vietnam through genuinely free and democratic general elections under international supervision. (c) Foreign countries shall not impose any political tendency or personality on the South Vietnamese people. [Chapter Four, Article Nine]

"The two South Vietnamese parties [meaning the Government of South Vietnam and the Viet Cong, which was also known by four other designations: the National Liberation Front for the Liberation of South Vietnam, the N.L.F., the Provisional Revolutionary Government, and the P.R.G.] undertake to respect the cease-fire and maintain peace in South Vietnam, settle all matters of contention through negotiations and avoid all armed conflict." [Chapter Four, Article Ten]

The best was yet to come in the following Article, in which we plagiarized a list of freedoms from our own First Amendment of the United States Constitution, with additions of even more freedoms than our Founders had itemized:

"Immediately after the cease-fire, the two South Vietnamese parties [The South Vietnam Government and the North Vietnam proxy: the Viet Cong] will: Achieve national reconciliation and concord, end hatred and enmity, prohibit all acts of reprisal and discrimination against individuals or organizations that have collaborated with one side or the other, insure the democratic liberties of the people: personal freedom, freedom of speech, freedom of the press, freedom of meeting, freedom of organization, freedom of political activities, freedom of belief, freedom of movement, freedom of residence, freedom of work, right to property ownership and right to free enterprise." [Chapter Four, Article Eleven]

* * *

And further within the Accords, there were guarantees to neighboring countries: "Foreign countries shall put an end to all military activities in Cambodia and Laos, totally withdraw from and refrain from reintroducing into these two countries troops, military advisers and military personnel, armaments, munitions and war material. The internal affairs of Cambodia and Laos shall be settled by the people of each of these countries without foreign interference." [Chapter Twenty, Article Twenty]

One of the most important provisions of the agreement was that "The two South Vietnam parties [South Vietnam and the Viet Cong] shall be permitted to make periodic replacement of armaments, munitions and war material which have been destroyed, damaged, worn out or used up after the cease-fire, on the basis of piece-for-piece," meaning the replacement of one helicopter for a helicopter, one gun for a gun, one bullet for a bullet: one replacement for one lost. [Chapter Four, Article Seven]

National Security Advisor Henry Kissinger explained, "There is a flat prohibition against the introduction of any military force into South Vietnam from outside of South Vietnam, which is to say that whatever forces may be in South Vietnam from outside South Vietnam, specifically North Vietnamese forces, cannot receive reinforcements, replacements or any other form of augmentation by any means whatsoever. With respect to military equipment, both sides are permitted to replace all existing military equipment on a one-to-one basis under international supervision and control."

* * *

The Paris Peace Accords were initialed for the United States by Henry Kissinger and initialed for North Vietnam by Le Duc Tho on January the 23rd, with signatures four days later on the 27th by William Rogers [U.S. Secretary of State], Tran Van Lam [South Vietnam's Minister of Foreign Affairs], Nguyen Duy Trinh [North Vietnam's Minister of Foreign Affairs], and Nguyen Thi Binh [the Viet Cong's Minister of Foreign Affairs].

All of this came about when—in pursuit of bringing the North Vietnamese back to the peace table in Paris after years of being on and off and on and off countless times since the Johnson Administration and into the Nixon Administration—President Nixon ordered the bombing of Hanoi and Haiphong, North Vietnam, in December of 1972 to force the North Vietnamese back to the Paris talks.

President Nixon had asked a number of those on his staff if they thought there should be a U.S. bombing pause for Christmas. He made it clear he favored such a pause for Christmas, but wanted their opinions. One of the responses to his request was, "Don't stop the bombing. The enemy will use any pause to increase their arms, regroup and realign themselves on the Ho Chi Minh Trail, and we'll pay the price. Besides, North Vietnam is an atheist-governed country that doesn't celebrate Christmas—not that the government there concerns itself with anyone's holiday. They used the truce of Tet—the Lunar New Year's Day in 1968—for their offensive against South Vietnam. I don't believe they should be trusted to take a Christmas holiday from their war."

The President overrode that opinion and followed his own instincts by calling for a 36-hour bombing pause for Christmas. That was of no consequence to many journalists, historians, and academics who referred to it (with many still referring to it) as "The Christmas Bombing."

The bombing had started on December 18, 1972, and after that intermission of 36 hours over Christmas, the bombing was re-started, then stopped on December 29 when the North Vietnamese agreed to resume peace talks in Paris. The President had also planned a 36-hour bombing pause for the New Year's Day holiday, but bombing had already stopped two days prior to the New Year. The Paris talks restarted on January 8, 1973. Before the month was done North Vietnam's signature was on the document of agreement.

Five weeks after the signing, an act of confirmation was signed [on March the 2nd] by the representatives of eleven nations plus the Viet Cong in the Act of the International Conference of Vietnam. [The eleven nations were Canada, France, Hungary, Indonesia, North Vietnam, People's Republic of China, Poland, United Kingdom, Union of Soviet Socialist Republics, United States of America, and South Vietnam.] The Act called for "respect of the Vietnamese people's fundamental national rights, and the South Vietnamese people's right to self determination . . . The Parties to this Act solemnly acknowledge the commitments by the parties to the Agreement and the Protocols to strictly respect and scrupulously implement the Agreement and the Protocols," and in the event of a violation, "the parties signatory to the Agreement and the Protocols shall, either individually or jointly, consult with the other Parties to this Act with a view to determining necessary remedial measures."

Most significantly, the Act was signed by Andrei Gromyko, the Minister of Foreign Affairs for the government of the

Union of Soviet Socialist Republics, and Chi Peng-Fei, the Minister for Foreign Affairs for the government of the People's Republic of China.

In the 40 days between the beginning of the bombing that brought about the Peace Accords and the signing of the Paris Peace Accords, the American people were told the following from prominent names in the U.S. media:

A *Washington Post* editorial commented that President Nixon conducted a bombing policy "so ruthless and so difficult to fathom politically, as to cause millions of Americans to cringe in shame and to wonder at their President's very sanity."

Joseph Kraft, a leading journalist whose syndicated columns appeared in newspapers throughout the nation, wrote: "Mr. Nixon called on the bombers—an action, in my judgment, of senseless terror which stains the good name of America."

Journalist James Reston, who was the Vice President of the *New York Times*, wrote: "This is war by tantrum."

The *New York Times* reported that waves of bombers "flying in wedges of three, lay down more than 65 tons of bombs at a time, in a carpet pattern one and one-half miles long and one mile wide ... the most intensive aerial bombardment in history ... equivalent to 20 of the atomic bombs dropped on Hiroshima." The *Times* informed its readers that all of this was occurring in "densely populated areas." [Hanoi's own figures, released at the time, put the total number of civilian casualties during the 12-day campaign at 1,300–1,600. The Hiroshima bombing referred to by the *New York Times* resulted in the deaths of 66,000 by the lowest estimate, with some estimates well over 100,000, far from the equivalence stated by the *New York Times*.] Four months later, after American military involvement in Vietnam was over, the *New York Times* admitted that "Hanoi Films Show No Carpet Bombing." Although it was late, it was corrected.

Dan Rather (CBS) told his audience that the United States "has embarked on a large-scale terror bombing," with the operative word "unrestricted." He quoted Hanoi to the effect that the strikes were "extermination raids on many populous areas."

Harry Reasoner (ABC) told his audience that "Dr. Kissinger's boss had broken Dr. Kissinger's word. It's very hard to swallow."

Eric Sevareid (CBS) told his audience, "In most areas of the government ... the feeling is one of dismay, tinged with shame that the United States is again resorting to mass killing in an effort to end the killing."

Walter Cronkite (CBS) told his audience that the "Soviet News Agency Tass said hundreds of U.S. bombers destroyed thousands of homes, most of them in the Hanoi-Haiphong area ... Hanoi Radio said the bombings indicate President Nixon has taken leave of his senses." He let the quote stand.

Anthony Lewis (the *New York Times*) wrote, "Even with sympathy for the men who fly American planes, and for their families, one has to recognize the greater courage of the North Vietnamese people . . . The elected leader of the greatest democracy acts like a maddened tyrant . . . To send B-52's against populous areas such as Hanoi or Haiphong can have only one purpose: terror. It was the response of a man so overwhelmed by his sense of inadequacy and frustration that he had to strike out, punish, destroy."

The major media had been unbalanced for some time, and they continued that imbalance. A study of the Institute for American

Strategy concluded that during 1972 and 1973, CBS News balance between favorable and unfavorable stories regarding U.S. military affairs was 13% favorable, 66.1% unfavorable. The study found that in 1972, 83.33% of themes in CBS stories about South Vietnam were critical of the Saigon government, while 57.32% about North Vietnam were favorable to the Hanoi government. Within the same year the study found that CBS quoted the statements of those who were critical of our policy 842 times, while those in favor of our policy were quoted 23 times.

Prominent among television specials on the war was the CBS presentation of a travelogue of North Vietnam narrated by John Hart of CBS, who reported from Hanoi:

"There is frequent laughter . . . Yesterday when I suggested that we'd like to get up early some morning to film the sunrise over one of these lakes, it was suggested that's a wonderful idea because after all, the American flyers cannot bomb the sun . . . Within a few hours of my arrival I have seen a richness in hospitality and a richness in hope . . . Five-thirty Sunday morning in Hanoi: This is the second Mass of the day. The cathedral is filled . . . American peace workers will be taken to see destroyed buildings and towns, and especially a number of destroyed or partially destroyed churches . . . There is a display of forgiveness by the villagers [toward captured pilots] . . . being released under the humanitarian policy of the government."

As Americans watched his films, a painting was shown and the painting was described as "recalling a bay . . . lovely . . . before it was heavily bombed." There were films of hospitals and churches allegedly bombed and damaged by Americans. There were no films of factories or bridges or railroads or supply centers bombed. No bombed war objectives of any sort were shown.

John Hart of CBS continued the travelogue with interviews of captured American prisoners of war, and through John Hart and through CBS their statements went into the homes of Americans, just as Hanoi wanted: "'I have been well treated since my capture and I would like to thank the people for their kindness . . . their humanity has also been shown by their release of three prisoners recently . . . I hope my government may soon bring this war to an end . . . To my family, my lovely wife, I would wish that they select the candidate they feel will stop this war.'"

On the evening of January the 23rd President Nixon made a televised address to the nation from the Oval Office of the White House, announcing the agreement made earlier that day in Paris: "In my addresses to the nation from this room on January 25 [1972] and May 8 [1972], I set forth the goals that we considered essential for peace with honor. In the settlement that has now been agreed to, all the conditions that I laid down then have been met—a cease-fire internationally supervised will begin at 7 p.m. this Saturday, January 27, Washington time. Within 60 days from this Saturday all Americans held prisoners of war throughout Indochina will be released.

"There will be the fullest possible accounting for all of those who are missing in action. During the same 60-day period all American forces will be withdrawn from South Vietnam.

"The people of South Vietnam have been guaranteed the right to determine their own future without outside interference.

"By joint agreement, the full text of the agreement and the protocols to carry it out will be issued tomorrow.

"Throughout these negotiations we have been in the closest consultation with President [Nguyen Van] Thieu and other representatives of the Republic of Vietnam [South Vietnam].

"This settlement meets the goals and has the full support of President Thieu and the government of the Republic of Vietnam as well as that of our other allies who are affected." [See Chapter Eight for details on this.]

"The United States will continue to recognize the government of the Republic of Vietnam as the sole legitimate government of South Vietnam. We shall continue to aid South Vietnam within the terms of the agreement, and we shall support efforts for the people of South Vietnam to settle their problems peacefully among themselves . . .

"Just yesterday, a great American who once occupied this office died. In his life, President Johnson endured the vilification of those who sought to portray him as a man of war, but there was nothing he cared about more deeply than achieving a lasting peace in the world.

"I remember the last time I talked with him. It was just the day after the New Year. He spoke then of his concern with bringing peace, with making it the right kind of peace. And I was grateful that he once again expressed his support for my efforts to gain such a peace. No one would have welcomed this peace more than he.

"And I know he would join me in asking for those who died and for those who live, let us consecrate this moment by resolving together to make the peace we have achieved a peace that will last.

"Thank you, and good evening."

* * *

And it *was* a good evening for those who, for so long, had pursued an end to North Vietnam's aggression. For many others, there was confusion as to how to greet the night. Many of them had joined demonstrations in which enemy flags had been waved. They held an investment in U.S. failure with their credibility hanging in the balance.

Before the night was done, Dick Moore said goodnight to the guard at the North-West Gate of the White House: "What a marvelous day, Al! And now what a marvelous night! You know the way the flag on the top of the residence is put at half-staff when some elected official dies?" [The residence is the White "House" itself, rather than any of the structures on the White House Compound that are used for offices.]

"Of course, Mr. Moore. It's always a sad sight to see it at half-staff. It happens too often." He looked back at the flag above the residence. "There it is at half-staff for L.B.J." Then he looked back at Dick Moore. "It's a month for a president. This time it never even had a chance to go back to full-staff from when Truman died—on the day after Christmas."

"Well, what's happening now with Vietnam is worthy of having the flag rise higher than it's ever been raised in our times. Above the top!" And he made a quick gesture of his head toward the half-staffed flag. "That's what we ought to do. Higher than it's ever been raised!"

Al looked confused and lowered his brows while shaking his head. "How do you do that? The flag is on a pole. How do you raise it above the top?"

"I don't know, Al. That's what you get paid for."

"*No* it isn't!"

Dick Moore's eyes were twinkling and that meant he intentionally was saying something outrageous so as to hear how his victim would respond. "Then who *does* get paid for it?"

"I don't know, Mr. Moore. Why don't you do it, sir? I'll tell the Secret Service you've been cleared to get up on the flagpole."

Dick Moore gave his jovial Irish smile that cheered anyone fortunate enough to see it. "Tomorrow, Al. I'll get up there tomorrow. I never like to climb that thing at night."

The President was careful not to use the word "victory" in his speech for obvious reasons that he detailed in later conversation: "I didn't want to rub their noses in it. Saving face is very important, particularly in that part of the world. Once we had their signatures—you don't give them reason to get their back up. And remember," and he hesitated, then added, "they hadn't yet released our men—the P.O.W.'s."

U.S. prisoners of war *were* released from North Vietnam; U.S. troops came home, and both Henry Kissinger of the United States and Le Duc Tho of North Vietnam received the Nobel Peace Prize for their negotiations of the Paris Peace Accords.

When the former prisoners of war disembarked from their rescue aircraft at Clark Air Force Base in the Philippines, there was genuine shock in America to hear their emotional statements in support of the U.S. mission of which they had been such an important part. The first off the aircraft was Captain Jeremiah Denton: "We are honored to have had the opportunity to serve our country under difficult circumstances. We are profoundly grateful to our Commander in Chief and to our

Nation for this day. And God Bless America." He was followed by a procession of others in varied physical condition, with some kissing the ground, some on crutches and stretchers unable to kiss the ground but kissing the air, and proclaiming their long-held and sustained support of U.S. policy. [See Chapter Ten]

President Nixon had earlier phoned Mrs. Lady Byrd Johnson and asked her if it would be alright with her if the first U.S. flag the returned prisoners of war would see at Clark Air Force Base would be at full-staff even though it was the period of time designated for all U.S. flags to be at half-staff in national mourning for the death of her husband. She said she wanted to think about it, but her thinking did not take long. Within minutes she phoned him back and said that with the former prisoners at last being in safety at a U.S. Air Force Base, she knew that her husband would not want them to be greeted with the flag of the United States flying in mourning, but rather flying at full-staff in welcoming them home.

In short time there were further statements from the returned former prisoners, including their belief that President Nixon's decision to bomb North Vietnam had been the best and only acceptable course. Some revealed that in Building 8 at Hoa Lo prison they not only heard the bombs dropping from B-52s but the walls were shaking with explosions and roars, and chunks of the ceiling's plaster fell over the floors. With each blast, the prisoners of war cheered. In Hoa Lo's Building 2, where a number of prisoners were together at the time, John Dramesi, Larry Guarino, Jim Kasler, Bob Shweitzer, and Ray Vohden not only cheered but danced. One episode after another was made known. [The Hoa Lo prison became known as the "Hanoi Hilton," and it was sarcastically renamed as "our home away from home" by Lt. Commander Everett "Ev" Alvarez, Jr., the longest-incarcerated U.S. prisoner of war during the Southeast Asian War.]

Captain Jeremiah Denton revealed, "On the night of 18 December 1972 at about 20:00 I heard a soft but growing humming noise, recognized it and shouted out, 'Boys, the war is over, those are B-52s!' Soon, the planes were overhead all around us. Sure enough that was the first night of Linebacker II [the December 1972 bombing of Hanoi and Haiphong, North Vietnam], consisting of three waves each of 80 B-52s in clear sight overhead, bombing the living hell out of North Vietnamese military targets . . . Falling flak made holes in the ceiling. It was quite an experience, but we were cheering all the time. The bombing started on the 18th, paused for Christmas, resumed on the 26th . . . The first night those B-52s flew in there, there were scores of missiles going up toward them and we lost a good number of B-52s. The next night, there may have been half as many missiles, and we lost half the number of B-52s. By the third night, maybe one or two B-52s were downed and very few missiles went up. From then on there was little or no missile opposition, and the planes methodically continued to come back unchallenged to bomb all the bridges, all the ammo dumps, power plants, the missile sites, etcetera—all of the infrastructure, military and industrial, of North Vietnam . . .

"Things changed abruptly when hundreds of bombs suddenly destroyed the Communist war-making potential, and bombs and crashing B-52s starting dropping around the leaders for the first time, threatening them with death. The leaders caved in completely by January 1973, knowing and admitting to me that they knew they had lost and were anxious to settle on our terms . . .

"They let us know that they thought that the war was over and I received my formal personal acknowledgement from them that they knew they had lost the war.

"We should have done in 1965 what we did finally in December 1972 and January 1973 in Operation Linebacker II.

"Because of Linebacker II, General Giap [General Vo Nguyen Giap, Commander in Chief of the People's Army of North Vietnam] and the rest of his officers and men totally lost that confidence and were more than prepared to end the war on our terms."

Yet two and one-quarter years after the Paris Peace Accords were signed, the government of South Vietnam surrendered to the government of North Vietnam, and the government of Cambodia surrendered to the Khmer Rouge.

What happened during those two and one-quarter years that forced their surrenders?

A great deal of importance happened, and so the American amnesia began with chapters from the following two and one-quarter years taken out of memory; the lack of remembrance enhanced by many academics and analysts who, for decades to come, would choose to ignore the truth on their papers and in their lectures. The truth would have been a testimony against their own advocacies and activities during the years of that war when they voiced opposition to the United States, and many of them had displayed their support for North Vietnam and for the Khmer Rouge of Cambodia, with that support having helped to bring about the defeat of those nations. Only the most courageous of them—and there are some—have said "I was wrong" to the new generations who didn't live through those times. Most of those who authored the amnesia hope the hiding of truth continues forever.

2

ENTER THE 94th U.S. CONGRESS

THE TWO AND one-quarter years began with North Vietnam and the Viet Cong receiving supplies from the Soviet Union on a four-to-one ratio in violation of the Paris Peace Accords. The United States stuck to the agreed-upon one-to-one ratio for re-supply to South Vietnam.

The then-current 93rd Congress, in violation of U.S. signatures, attempted to stop *any* aid to the governments of South Vietnam and Cambodia. This was done by adding anti-aid riders in the form of amendments to bills that were unrelated to the war. These included the Eagleton Amendment and the Case-Church Amendment that passed by veto-proof majorities disallowing any funds to go toward military involvement in Southeast Asia without prior congressional approval. Then there was the passage by the Congress of the War Powers Act, which was not a rider but a separate bill. The President vetoed it, but his veto was overridden by the Congress. [See Chapter Eleven.] All of this gave confidence to the North Vietnamese Government that it could do what it wanted to do without fear of U.S. military action, unless President Nixon disobeyed the new laws passed by the Congress.

Additionally, with the help of the Soviet Union and the People's Republic of China, North Vietnam continued to send troops and equipment into Cambodia, also in violation of the Paris Peace Accords. In response, the United States continued its air interdiction, bombing those areas used by North Vietnam within Cambodia.

The air interdiction by the United States on Cambodian territory invaded by North Vietnam had been going on for periods of time prior to the Paris Peace Accords, and now the 93rd Congress [composed of 234 Democrats, 191 Republicans in House membership, and 57 Democrats, 43 Republicans in the Senate] attempted to have them stopped, saying that our troops no longer needed to be protected in South Vietnam since our troops were no longer there, having left in compliance with the Paris Peace Accords. The Administration argued that the Congress was hand-picking its argument since the Congress was totally aware that it had previously authorized such strikes not only to protect U.S. troops but also for two other objectives: to protect South Vietnam from North Vietnamese infiltration, which was continuing by North Vietnam using Cambodian territory as a staging ground to move into South Vietnam, and to protect the Cambodian Government from both the North Vietnamese and the Khmer Rouge.

As in previous cases, the Congress put their argument in the form of a rider on a funding bill for the United States Government. It passed the Congress on June 25, 1973.

President Nixon vetoed the bill with the statement: "I am returning today without my approval H.R. 7447, the Second Supplemental Appropriation Act of 1973 . . . After more than ten arduous years of suffering and sacrifice in Indochina, an equitable framework for peace was finally agreed to in Paris last January. We are now involved in concluding the last element of that settlement: a Cambodian settlement. It would be nothing short of tragic if this great accomplishment, bought with the blood of so many Asians and Americans, were to be undone now by Congressional action . . . A Communist victory in Cambodia, in turn, would threaten the fragile balance of negotiated agreements, political alignments and military capabilities upon which the overall peace in Southeast Asia depends and on which my assessment of the acceptability of the Vietnam agreements was based.

"Finally, and with even more serious global implications, the legislatively imposed acceptance of the United States to Communist violations of the Paris agreements and the conquest of Cambodia by Communist forces would call into question our national commitment not only to the Vietnam settlement but to many other settlements or agreements we have reached or seek to reach with other nations. A serious blow to America's international credibility would have been struck—a blow that would be felt far beyond Indochina . . .

"However, I must emphasize that the provisions of H.R. 7447, other than the 'Cambodia rider,' contain a number of appropriations that are essential to the continuity of governmental operations. It is critical that these appropriations be enacted immediately. By June 28, nine Government agencies will have exhausted their authority to pay the salaries and expenses of their employees. The disruptions that would be caused by a break in the continuity of government are serious and must be prevented. For example, it will be impossible to meet the payroll of the employees at the Social Security Administration, which will threaten to disrupt the flow of benefits to 25 million persons. But an even greater disservice to the American people—and to all other peace loving people—would be the enactment of a measure which would seriously undermine the chances for a lasting peace in Indochina and jeopardize our efforts to create a stable, enduring structure of peace around the world. It is to prevent such a destructive development that I am returning H.R. 7447 without my approval."

The veto was upheld. The rider was eliminated from the funding bill. The Administration won—but not for long.

The controversy between the executive and the legislative branches of government went on with further legislation promised by the Congress. Simultaneously the issue was brought to the Judiciary by Elizabeth Holtzman, Congressman from New York [in *Holtzman v. Schlesinger*, against Secretary of Defense James Schlesinger]. The judicial journey never made it to the Supreme Court because before it was reviewed, the Congress and the Administration made a compromise agreement. (It was a compromise the President later regretted having made.) The bombing would be halted on August the 15th, which would give the President some six weeks to continue the air interdiction against the North Vietnamese in Cambodia, but with a strict cut-off after the six weeks. Without the compromise, the President was warned the Congress would add a "Cambodia rider" to any and every appropriation bill, meaning that if the President didn't sign any of those bills, essential workings of government would be brought to a halt. It was a form of now-familiar legislative blackmail.

Then came the most important chapters within the two and one-quarter years between the Paris Peace Accords and the surrenders of Cambodia and South Vietnam.

First, the Watergate scandal [that had taken place on June 17, 1972] escalated into massive national prominence in 1973 and brought about the resignation of President Nixon from office on August 9, 1974, in the greatest political victory for an opposition party in our nation's history.

Then, less than three months after the transition of the presidency from Nixon to Ford, came the congressional elections of 1974 [November the 5th of 1974]. It was a landslide of immense proportions for the Democrats [giving the new House of Representatives a total of 291 Democrats and 144 Republicans, and a Senate membership of 61 Democrats and 39 Republicans].

The outgoing 93rd Congress was only the overture before the curtain rose to present the new 94th Congress. When it convened on January the 3rd, 1975, President Ford became no more than a caretaker President, as the Congress ran not only the legislative branch of government but successfully attempted to run foreign affairs of the executive branch, taking from this President his constitutional role as Commander in Chief. In greater acceleration than the previous Congress, one piece of legislation after another was drafted to stop his powers in giving promised aid to South Vietnam and Cambodia, no matter what we had promised in the Paris Peace Accords, and no matter what reminders of those promises had been made in letters to President Thieu from President Nixon on behalf of the United States. [See Chapter Eight.]

Eleven days after the 94th Congress convened, Secretary of Defense James Schlesinger testified to the new Congress that the United States had made a promise to President Thieu of South Vietnam that if the North Vietnamese violated the Paris Accords we would respond with severe retaliatory action, and we could not be guilty of violating our signature.

The anti–U.S. policy advocates around the nation had turned into a powerful lobby that not even the signed Paris Peace Accords had been able to stop. To be opposed to United Sates policy in Southeast Asia had become a "semi-career" of many. But since the signing of the Accords, all they had left was the choice of admitting U.S. victory or having it reversed. They encouraged the 94th Congress to increase its efforts to stop all U.S. aid to South Vietnam so there would be no economic funds provided and no re-supply of military equipment that South Vietnam had lost. Simultaneously, there came demands to the 94th Congress to reject any and all aid to the Cambodian Government, while the Khmer Rouge, led by Pol Pot, received more and more aid from the People's Republic of China, although the People's Republic of China had signed the Act of the International Conference of Vietnam that approved the Paris Peace Accords.

Throughout the beginning of 1975, both Cambodia and South Vietnam were undergoing heavy military offenses from their Communist enemies.

On April the 4th of 1975, General Fred C. Weyand, the U.S.

Army Chief of Staff, sent a memorandum classified as secret, followed by a 15-page report, also classified as secret, to President Ford. Excerpts follow from General Weyand's memo and report that comprise one of the most itemized, direct, and passionately written communications between a General to a U.S. President in contemporary times. These excerpts are long, but are too important for any further redaction:

4 April 1975

MEMORANDUM FOR THE PRESIDENT

Subject: Vietnam Assessment

In accordance with your instructions, I visited South Vietnam during the period 28 March–4 April. I have completed my assessment of the current situation there, analyzed what the Government of the Republic of Vietnam intends to do to counter the aggression from the North, assured President Thieu of your steadfast support in this time of crisis, and examined the options and actions open to the United States to assist the South Vietnamese.

The current military situation is critical, and the probability of the survival of South Vietnam as a truncated nation in the northern province is marginal at best. The GVN [Government of South Vietnam] is on the brink of a total military defeat. However, the South is planning to continue to defend with their available resources, and, if allowed respite, will rebuild their capabilities to the extent that United States support in material will permit. I believe that we owe them that support . . .

* * *

The present level of U.S. support guarantees GVN defeat. Of the $700 million provided for FY 1975 [Fiscal Year 1975 having started on July the 1st, 1974. The starting of Fiscal Years on October the 1st was not in effect until 1976], the remaining $150 million can be used for a very short time for a major supply operation; however, if there is to be any real chance of success, an additional $272 million is urgently needed to bring the South Vietnamese to a minimal defense posture to meet the Soviet and PRC [People's Republic of China] supported invasion. Additional U.S. aid is within both the spirit and intent of the Paris agreement, which remains the practical framework for a peaceful settlement in Vietnam ...

United States credibility as an ally is at stake in Vietnam. To sustain that credibility we must take a maximum effort to support the South Vietnamese now.

A more detailed analysis is contained in the attached report ...

[From the report] The Paris Agreement of 27 January 1973 marked not the beginning of peace in Vietnam, but instead the beginning of a Communist build-up of supplies and equipment for continued North Vietnamese military aggression in Vietnam. In the ensuing 26 months since the Agreement was signed, North Vietnam rebuilt the Ho Chi Minh Trail into a major all-weather supply artery. They built pipelines extending 330 miles into South Vietnam ... With this major supply system in full operation, they quadrupled their field artillery, greatly increased their anti-aircraft and sent six times as much armor into South Vietnam as they had in January 1973. At the same time, they increased their troop strength by almost 200,000 men. All of these actions were in direct violation of the Paris Agreement. The U.S., by contrast, did not fulfill its obligations to maintain South Vietnamese equipment and materials as they were authorized to do under the Agreement. Ground ammunition declined from 179 thousand short tons at the cease fire to 126 thousand short tons when the current NVA [North Vietnamese Army] offensive began . . .

The historical record outlined above set the stage for the current situation in South Vietnam . . .

In mid-February, President Thieu sent Senator Tran Van Lam to the U.S. as a private emissary to assess the mood of Congress with respect to Vietnam and the prospects for favorable Congressional action on aid legislation. Lam submitted a very pessimistic appraisal, which Thieu felt was confirmed by the early March votes of the House Democratic caucus . . . Thieu saw his country faced with a major Communist offensive coinciding with a curtailment, and possible cessation, of U.S. aid. He and his military advisors therefore decided that a drastic strategic retrenchment was essential to the GVN's survival . . .

Communist forces have the momentum of success and though they have suffered casualties, which may have been heavy, they are being augmented daily by fresh replacements and supplies from North Vietnam. During the last three weeks in March, five ARVN [Army of the Republic of (South) Vietnam] divisions, twelve Ranger Groups and two brigade equivalents of armor have been rendered combat ineffective. Officers and men from these units can be regrouped into new formations, but virtually all of their equipment has been lost. Many other GVN units have suffered heavy losses in personnel and equipment . . .

From the time the Paris Agreement was signed in 1973, Hanoi has been steadily improving its military capabilities in South Vietnam through a continuous improvement of its logistic infrastructure (roads, trails, depots, etc., in both Laos and South Vietnam) and a continuous infusion of supplies, equipment and troops—all in direct violation of Article 7 of the 1973 Agreement. This flow has peaked and valleyed over the past 26 months, but it has never stopped.

In the summer of 1974, when the GVN's overall position looked promising, this manpower and supply augmenting North Vietnam's invading expeditionary force in the South was down. It began to pick up soon after last summer's political developments within the United States [reaction to Watergate and U.S. presidential transition] and diminishing Congressional support for continued assistance to South Vietnam. The logistic flow of men and matériel out of North Vietnam—and, hence, the North Vietnam Army's capabilities in the south—began to pick up in the latter part of 1974. The pace has been intense since the beginning of 1975, was increased in February and March, and is now going at full throttle.

* * *

Hanoi certainly had planned a significant level of offensive action this spring. In retrospect, the "Phase I" January campaign (which overran Phuoc Long Province), among other things, seems to have been a test of whether the U.S. would react to what even Hanoi must have considered a blatant violation of the 1973 Paris Agreement . . .

How much Hanoi's goals may have escalated or its appetite been whetted by the past month's events in South Vietnam—and in the United States—is impossible to tell, particularly since even Hanoi has not had time to digest the most recent developments. The rate at which men and supplies are coming from North Vietnam into South Vietnam, however, certainly suggests that Hanoi intends to keep pressing its invading expeditionary force's attacks . . .

One of the most serious psychological and attitudinal problems at all levels, military and civilian, is the belief that the South Vietnamese have been abandoned, and even betrayed, by the United States. The Communists are using every possible device of propaganda and psychological warfare to foster this view. The higher one goes in the social or hierarchical scale, the greater the degree of sharpness and focus to such sentiments. Much of this emotion is keyed on the 1973 Paris Agreement and subsequent U.S. withdrawal. It is widely believed that the GVN was forced to sign this agreement as a result of a private U.S.–North Vietnam deal under which the U.S. was allowed to withdraw its forces and get its prisoners back in return for abandoning South Vietnam. This sense of abandonment has been intensified by what is widely perceived as a lack of public U.S. acknowledgement of South Vietnam's current plight or willingness to provide needed support . . .

What happens in South Vietnam over the next month or so, let alone a longer time frame, depends very much on what is done—or not done—by North Vietnam, the GVN, and the United States during the next two to three weeks and even the next few days . . .

The action which the U.S. could take which would have the greatest immediate effect on Vietnamese perceptions—North and South—would be the use of U.S. air power to blunt the current NVA offensive. Even if confined to South Vietnam and carried out for only a limited time, such attacks would take a severe toll on the North Vietnamese expeditionary force's manpower and supplies, and have a dramatic morale impact on North Vietnam's invading troops. These attacks would also give Hanoi's leaders pause, and raise concerns which do not now exist, about the risks involved in ignoring a formal agreement made with the United States.

South Vietnamese military leaders at all levels have repeatedly cited the importance of B-52 attacks to the conduct of a successful defense against superior enemy forces, and there is sound military justification for such a point of view.

The above comments convey only a military assessment. I recognize, however, the significant legal and political implications which would attend the exercise of such an action.

One important step that the U.S. should take is to make it clear that the U.S. supports South Vietnam . . .

This effort could stress three principal themes:

The Vietnamese people, with first-hand knowledge of life under both the Thieu Government and communism, have clearly indicated their choice by "voting with their feet," as the East Germans did before the introduction of the Berlin Wall. The mass exodus from the northern provinces, in the face of hardships, danger and intense human suffering, is a true sign of their feelings. In their choice, none have fled north to Hanoi and North Vietnam—where there is no fighting, where there are no refugee columns, and where war has not touched since the Paris Agreement. The question is not an academic one to the individual Vietnamese; it is one of life and death. By their actions they have chosen liberty and possible death.

South Vietnam is fighting a <u>defensive</u> war. U.S. material is used to defend South Vietnam, while Soviet and Chinese tanks and war material are being used by the North Vietnamese for open, naked, defiant aggression. It is this North Vietnamese invasion, not the actions of the South Vietnamese, that has already required the Administration to seek additional support from the Congress.

We should continue to emphasize the effect of Vietnam on the credibility of any U.S. commitment. The world clearly understands past U.S. commitments to Vietnam. Our expenditure of lives and resources in pursuit of this commitment is well known to all. The governments of the world know the past, but will see any present inability to support the Vietnamese in their crisis of survival as a failure of U.S. will and resolve. If we make no effort, our future credibility as perceived by ally and potential adversary alike will be lost for years to come.

Statements of U.S. support are important, but it is also essential that the message be validated with concrete actions to demonstrate that the United States stands behind her ally. While the ultimate availability of military resources will rest with supplemental appropriations in the Congress for the current fiscal year, there is more than $150 million available from the $700 million voted in the Defense Appropriations Act. This money can be used to meet the most immediate needs now and in the next few weeks. However, the rapid expenditure of the remaining funds will soon exhaust U.S. capabilities to provide support. A supplemental appropriations bill, probably for $722 million, is urgently needed for basic military necessities to provide a chance for the survival of the Republic of Vietnam . . .

The President acted quickly: Six days after General Weyand's memo and report were written, President Ford went before an evening Joint Session of the Congress [April the 10th, 1975] to literally beg for a package of U.S. aid. It was broadcast live on radio and television. Excerpts from his speech to the 94th Congress follow:

"A vast human tragedy has befallen our friends in Vietnam and Cambodia ... The chances for an enduring peace after the last American fighting man left Vietnam in 1973 rested on two publicly stated premises: First, that if necessary, the United States would help sustain the terms of the Paris accords it signed two years ago, and second, that the United States would provide adequate economic and military assistance to South Vietnam ... The situation in South Vietnam and Cambodia has reached a critical phase requiring immediate and positive decisions by this Government. The options before us are few and the time is very short ... I am therefore asking the Congress to appropriate without delay 722 million dollars for emergency military assistance and an initial sum of 250 million dollars for economic and humanitarian aid for South Vietnam ... [A total of 972 million dollars.]

"In Cambodia, the situation is tragic ... And yet, for the past three months, the beleaguered people of Phnom Penh have fought on, hoping against hope that the United States would not desert them, but instead provide the arms and ammunition they so badly needed ... In January, I requested food and ammunition for the brave Cambodians, and I regret to say that as of this evening, it may soon be too late ...

"Let no potential adversary believe that our difficulties or our debates mean a slackening of our national will. We will stand by our friends, we will honor our commitments, and we will uphold our country's principles."

But we didn't.

* * *

Some members of the Congress walked out on the President's speech in protest.

Senator Mark Hatfield said he was "appalled that a man could continue in such a bankrupt policy."

House Majority Leader, Representative Thomas (Tip) O'Neil, said that congressional approval was inconceivable as "there would have to be a complete turnaround" of public opinion to support such aid.

Representative Phil Burton called President Ford's proposal for aid "an outrage."

Senator Henry Jackson said, "It's dead. I oppose it."

One week after President Ford's rejected plea to the 94th Congress, Cambodia fell [April 17, 1975], followed thirteen days later by the fall of South Vietnam [April 30, 1975].

Some of the April events in those two countries follow.

3

THE APRIL SURRENDERS

THE U.S. ECONOMIC pipeline became totally hollow while even a more massive avalanche of supplies multiplied from the People's Republic of China to the Khmer Rouge in Cambodia, and from the Soviet Union and the People's Republic of China to the North Vietnam Army, including the Viet Cong in South Vietnam, and to the Pathet Lao (the Communist forces) in Laos.

Long Beret, the Premier of Cambodia said, "We have no more material means" to continue, and "we feel completely abandoned."

U.S. Ambassador John Gunther Dean offered evacuation and refuge to Cambodian officials. Prince Sirik Matak of Phnom Penh wrote a letter to U.S. Ambassador Dean on April 12, 1975, five days before the fall of that capital city of Cambodia, in which he wrote:

Dear Excellency and Friend,

I thank you very sincerely for your letter and for your offer to transport me towards freedom. I cannot, alas, leave in such a cowardly fashion. As for you and in particular for your great country, I never believed for a moment that you would have this sentiment of abandoning a people which has chosen liberty. You have refused us your protection and we can do nothing about it. You leave us and it is my wish that you and your country will find happiness under the sky. But mark it well that, if I shall die here on the spot and in my country that I love, it is too bad because we are all born and must die one day. I have only committed the mistake of believing in you, the Americans.

Please accept, Excellency, my dear friend, my faithful and friendly sentiments.

Sirik Matak.

Prince Matak was reported to have been executed four days after the fall of Phnom Penh as the genocide began.

On April the 17th, 1975, the Cambodian Government surrendered. The Khmer Rouge came into the capital city of Phnom Penh and ordered its immediate evacuation as well as ordering the evacuation of all other urban areas of Cambodia. Surgeries in progress at Preah Ket Mealea Hospital were ordered stopped and the doctors, nurses, and those undergoing surgery were either executed or ordered out of the hospital for their journey into the fields. Those who were not in surgery but did not rise fast enough on orders were murdered in their beds. Similar events were told about other hospitals throughout the country as far away from Phnom Penh as Siem Reap. Within that one day over 3 million people were herded to march into the countryside at risk of death if they stopped walking. On the trek to the fields it was a capital offense to complain to guards about the food. It was a capital offense to talk to one another.

The next day all married couples were separated, their children taken away or compelled to watch their parents tortured and executed, often by decapitation, while the chief method of execution was to have the person's skull smashed by hammer. Bullets were considered to be too precious to be wasted on such things. Children were forced to watch their parents lined up with others, each person in each row having their skulls smashed by Khmer Rouge with hammers, and the same fate came later for selected children.

For those living, all family names were changed and their birth-names forbidden from use so that none could locate other members of their families.

Most of those found to have served in the previous government were executed, as were their wives or husbands. The designation 'S-21' became a more dreaded designation than death. It was quickly known as the name of the Khmer Rouge's torture chamber in Phnom Penh. 'S-21' had previously been a high school called Tuol Sleng. It was later learned that of some 16,000 imprisoned in 'S-21', less than 20 people survived.

Public executions were held throughout the country, and starvation was rampant. All street signs were whitewashed. All money was declared illegal, with rice as the only currency. Medical facilities, religious temples, postal, telegraph, and telephone communications were destroyed. Death was the sentence for having a radio or having any timepiece or dozing at work. Flirting was considered to be promiscuity punishable by death. All people had to wear black tops and black pants. Atheism was the new official creed, with the practices of Buddhism and Catholicism punishable by death. All books published before April 17, 1975 were ordered to be burned. In a quest for extinction of lives, the genocide of an estimated 2 million (somewhere between one-quarter to one-third of the entire population of the country) began on that date.

But statistics tell nothing but numbers. Each story told with detail and unstoppable tears by those who survived are unthinkable. No fiction writer, no matter how sadistic, could imagine such things.

Only eight foreign embassies remained: the People's Republic of China, North Korea, Cuba, Albania, Laos, Romania, Yugoslavia, and Egypt.

In the week *previous* to Cambodia's surrender, the American people were audience to the following words and advice from the 94th Congress as it evaluated President Ford's plea for aid to prevent surrender:

Senator George McGovern said, "Cambodians would be better off if we stopped all aid to them and let them work things out in their own way."

Congressman Donald Fraser was asked if he wanted Cambodia to surrender. He answered, "Yes, under controlled circumstances to minimize the loss of life."

Congressman [later to become Senator] Chris Dodd said, "The greatest gift our country can give to the Cambodian people is not guns but peace, and the best way to accomplish that goal is by ending military aid now."

Congressman Milton (Bob) Carr said, "If we really want to help the people of Cambodia and the people of South Vietnam, is it not wiser to end the killing?"

Congressman Tom Downey said, "It is time that we allow the peaceful people of Cambodia to rebuild their nation."

Senator Majority Leader Mike Mansfield said, "The cut-off of aid is in the best interest of Cambodians."

In addition, many analysts in the media were allies of the 94th Congress in the *pre*-surrender debate.

Anthony Lewis, in his syndicated column, wrote that continued American aid to Cambodia could "only prolong the agony of Cambodia ... What future could be more terrible than the reality of what is happening to Cambodia now?"

A *New York Times* editorial noted that further aid to Cambodia would "only extend Cambodia's misery."

Joseph Kraft wrote in his syndicated column, "Does it really matter whether Cambodia goes communist? The price is small."

Sidney Schanberg, who was later glorified in the 1984 film *The Killing Fields*, wrote directly from Southeast Asia: "I have seen the Khmer Rouge and they are not killing anyone ... Wars nourish brutality and sadism and sometimes certain people are executed by the victors, but it would be tendentious to forecast such abnormal behavior as a national policy under a communist government once the war is over." [In 1976 Sidney Schanberg won the Pulitzer Prize for his reporting in Cambodia.]

Tom Wicker wrote there was "not much moral choice" between the Lon Nol Government and the communists.

Four days before the genocide began, an article in the *New York Times* was titled, "Indochina Without Americans: For Most a Better Life."

Then South Vietnam:

President Ford held a question-and-answer session regarding South Vietnam at the Annual Convention of the American Society of Newspaper Editors on April 16, 1975 [the day prior to the fall of Cambodia and two weeks before the surrender of South Vietnam]. Excerpts follow:

THE PRESIDENT: " . . . In the agreement that was signed in Paris in January of 1973, the United States, as part of its agreement with South Vietnam, agreed to supply replacement war matériel, to give economic aid. The Soviet Union and the People's Republic of China, I assume, made the same commitment to North Vietnam. It appears that they have maintained that commitment. Unfortunately, the United States did not carry out its commitment in the supplying of military hardware and economic aid to South Vietnam. I wish we had. I think if we had, this present tragic situation in South Vietnam would not have occurred. But I don't think we can blame the Soviet Union and the People's Republic of China in this case. If we had done with our ally what we promised, I think this whole tragedy could have been eliminated. But nevertheless, we hope to and are working through the countries that are a part or were a part of the Paris Accords to try and achieve a cease-fire, and will continue to do so."

QUESTION: "On that point, you have asked for more than 700 million dollars worth of military aid. Now, there is some obvious psychological and symbolic reason for simply asking, but militarily speaking, if you could get the package through Congress and get it to South Vietnam, would it militarily do any good at this point?"

THE PRESIDENT: "I am absolutely convinced if Congress made available 722 million dollars in military assistance in a timely way by the date that I have suggested—or sometime shortly thereafter—the South Vietnamese could stabilize the military situation in South Vietnam today."

QUESTION: "Mr. President, you have talked a great deal about the moral obligation of this country to provide more military arms for South Vietnam. But what about the moral obligation to the suffering people of that country; the moral obligation to end that war?"

THE PRESIDENT: "Well, Mr. Reston, the agreement which was signed, I think, by twelve nations in January of 1973 in Paris—and I was there; I saw the signing was accomplished with the expectation that that war would end. If the agreement had been lived up to, the war would not now be going on. We have continued in various ways to try and achieve a cease-fire, and I can assure you that we intend to continue those efforts. But it is tragic, in my judgment, that what everybody thought was good in January of 1973 has been violated, and now we are faced with a terrible catastrophe at the present time."

QUESTION: "But would we not then, a year from now or five years from now, still have the same moral obligation you speak of?"

THE PRESIDENT: "Well, it is my best judgment, based on experts within the Administration, both economic and military, that if we had made available for the next three years reasonable sums of military aid and economic assistance, that South Vietnam would have been viable, that it could have met any of its economic problems, could have met any military challenges. This is another of the tragedies. For just a relatively small additional commitment in economic and military aid, relatively small compared to the 150 billion that we spent, that at the last minute of the last quarter we don't make that special effort, and now we are faced with this human tragedy. It just makes me sick every day I hear about it, read about it, and see it."

As the fall of South Vietnam became more and more imminent, the *New York Times* editorialized that "North Vietnam is obviously acting in massive violation of the military provisions of the 1973 truce, but President Thieu has just as clearly violated the political provisions of that accord—the procedures for establishing a coalition National Council [with the Viet Cong] to create a new political constitution for South Vietnam. Even now spokesmen for North Vietnam and its ally in the south, the Provisional Revolutionary Government [the Viet Cong], are insisting that their immediate goal is to implement these provisions and thereby avoid one final battle in the streets of Saigon."

The CBS Evening News reported on April 15, 1975, the fight for Xuan Loc, 40 miles east of Saigon, with Bob Simon stating that the battle of Xuan Loc was a symbol of South Vietnam's will to resist and "a symbol of North Vietnam's determination to end the war this year, perhaps this month." Aggressors and defenders became blurred. Although Bob Simon's narrative might have been intended to display that he was even-handed without bias, his words revealed the opposite. The North Vietnamese determination was not simply to *end* the war. That could have been accomplished decades back by not having pursued a takeover of South Vietnam. *More* recently the North Vietnamese could have ended the war by simply observing the agreement they signed in January of 1973. On the other side, South Vietnam never had any ambition to have jurisdiction over North Vietnam. Its only ambition was to successfully defend itself against North Vietnam's war to gain jurisdiction over South Vietnam.

With surrender in sight, on April the 21st, President Thieu resigned as President of South Vietnam. On resignation night he gave a television and radio address to his nation in which he said, "At the time of the peace agreement, the United States agreed to replace equipment on a one-by-one basis. But the United States did not keep its word. Is an American's word reliable these days? . . . The United States did not keep its promise to help us fight for freedom, and it was in the same fight that the United States lost 50,000 of its young men . . . The United States has not respected its promises. It is inhumane. It is untrustworthy. It is irresponsible." [President Thieu left for Taiwan, transferring the Presidency to Vice President Tran Van Huong. Within one week, on April 28, Tran Van Huong handed the office to the more neutral General Duong Minh, known as "Big Minh."]

* * *

As it became more and more obvious that the United States would not intervene, Americans in South Vietnam were given the secret plans for quick evacuation should it become necessary.

Time magazine put the contingency plans into world view in the Monday, May 5 edition, which was on newsstands on Monday, April 28: "The Pentagon made contingency plans for an all too conceivable eventuality: the closing of Tan Son Nhut [Saigon's Airport and Air Base] by Communist troops or the lethal SA-2 and SA-7 missiles that were being positioned near the airfield. This operation—known as Phase Two—would be carried out by more than 60 giant CH-46 and CH-53 helicopters. The choppers would whirl in from the decks of the U.S. aircraft carriers Hancock, Okinawa, and Midway, now standing off South Vietnam as part of a veritable armada of more than 40 vessels, including two other carriers.

"All Americans in Saigon were advised last week that the May-Day signal for Phase Two would be a weather report for Saigon of '105 and rising' broadcast over the American Radio Service, followed by the playing of several bars of 'White Christmas' at 15-minute intervals. That message would send the last Americans still in Saigon streaming toward 13 'LZs,' or landing zones situated throughout the downtown district, all atop U.S. owned or operated buildings . . . "

The phone rang at a little before 8:00 in the evening of the 28th at the D.C. residence of Robert Caruthers, who used to work at the White House. There was some static and some echoing, but it was recognizable as the distinctive voice of the twelve -or thirteen-year-old daughter of a friend in Saigon who had been helpful to the U.S. Military Command Assistance Vietnam

[MACV]. He often had his daughter with him to act as an interpreter, since she was much more proficient in English (and French) than he was.

"Mr. Caruthers?"

"Yes."

"This is Ahn."

"Ahn Pham?"

"Yes. Ahn Pham."

"Where are you calling from?"

"Saigon."

"At the Embassy?"

"No. Home. There is a curfew now all the time. Not just night. Now day, too. It is night where you are but it is morning here. I put in this call so much time ago in the night. Now it is morning."

"Are you safe?"

"No. No one is safe here."

He was silent for a while. "Are you with your mother and father?"

"Yes. They are here. They wanted me to phone you."

"Oh, Ahn! You and your parents should get to the Embassy!"

"Is America going to take care of us?"

"Ahn, we must! Yes, we must!"

"Will you help, Mr. Caruthers?"

"I will do what I can from here, but I don't know what I can do. You must get to the Embassy."

"No. They don't want us anymore. Are they going to let Saigon fall?"

He didn't know how to respond. "I don't know what we can or can't do, Ahn. Can you get to the Embassy?"

"It is not like it was before when you were here the last time. Everything has changed. It is all changed now. Even the streets. Everyone is running. Everyone is different than before."

"Ahn, let me see if I can do anything at all. I don't have much—much—I don't work at the White House anymore. So I don't know what's going on. Ignore the curfew. It is important that you get to the Embassy. Or to JUSPAO [Joint U.S. Public Affairs Office]. Even to Tan Son Nhut. That's it—go to the airport. Yes, you and your parents go to the airport!"

"Then you are saying we are going to fall?"

"I am not saying anything other than what I am saying! Listen to me, Ahn! Listen to me! Yes, if you can't get to the Embassy or JUSPAO, go to the airport. Don't try to bring things. No possessions. Just you and your mother and father. Just get there. Now! Go!"

"I don't think we can. The streets are different. There is—there is panic here. Is that the word?"

"Get there, please!"

At the same time, across the hall from the Oval Office in the Roosevelt Room at the White House, President Ford was meeting with his National Security Council. The meeting had started at 7:23 in the evening with its ten participants sitting at the room's conference table. [The participants were the President, Vice President Nelson Rockefeller, Secretary of State Henry Kissinger, Secretary of Defense James Schlesinger, Chairman of the Joint Chiefs of Staff General George Brown, Director of the C.I.A., William Colby, Deputy Secretary of State Robert Ingersoll, Deputy Secretary of Defense William Clements, National Security Advisor Brent Scowcroft, and W.R. Smyser, Senior Staff

Member of the National Security Council.] From the minutes, some pertinent excerpts from the 45-minute meeting follow:

PRESIDENT FORD: "Brent Scowcroft this afternoon brought me the report that two Marines had been lost, so I felt we should convene the National Security Council to discuss the situation in Saigon. Who can bring us up to date?"

C.I.A. DIRECTOR COLBY: "I think I can. What has happened is that the Viet Cong have rejected Minh's cease-fire offer. They have now added a third demand which is to dismantle the South Vietnamese armed forces. Bien Hoa is in the process of falling. The Viet Cong have cut off the road to the Delta and are advancing on Vung Tau. It is a very dangerous situation. The North Vietnamese are bringing artillery within range of Tan Son Nhut airport. At 4:00 a.m. they had a salvo of rockets against Tan Son Nhut. That is what killed the Marines. This salvo was followed by 120 millimeter artillery fire. Some of this artillery fire hit the American side, not the Vietnamese side last night." . . .

PRESIDENT FORD: "Has the rocket and the other fire now stopped?"

C.I.A. DIRECTOR COLBY: "No. It is continuing." . . .

SECRETARY OF STATE KISSINGER: "I have talked to [Ambassador] Graham Martin. I think the DAO [U.S. Defense Attaché Office at Tan Son Nhut airport] should come out anyway. I also think the Embassy should be thinned down. If we have to go to suppressive fire, then we must remove the Americans. Otherwise, it is too risky."

SECRETARY OF DEFENSE SCHLESINGER: "There is no authority now for suppressive fire, only for the chopper lift." . . .

CHAIRMAN OF THE JOINT CHIEFS OF STAFF BROWN: "I think they [the North Vietnamese] have pulled out the stops. The platoons that we have spoken of are being followed by more. They came in through that same area during the Tet offensive. They are ready for the battle of Tan Son Nhut."

PRESIDENT FORD: "If we decide on air cover, we have to go for the evacuation of Saigon and not just Tan Son Nhut. How soon will we know if the C-130s can land?"

CHAIRMAN OF THE JOINT CHIEFS OF STAFF BROWN: "Within an hour. We have an open line to Graham Martin."

SECRETARY OF STATE KISSINGER: "I think we have three decisions: First, how long to operate, and whether the C-130s should just pull out Americans or Vietnamese as well. In either event, today is clearly the last day for fixed-wing operations. Second, whether you want to have air cover flown over Tan Son Nhut or wherever the evacuees can be picked up. Third, when we order suppressive fire. In this connection, I agree with Jim that it should only be used when pulling out Americans. My concern is in balancing the risk to pull out all the stops if they have not yet decided to do so. I think if they see American air cover it would have a good effect." ...

N.S.C. ADVISOR SCOWCROFT: "We have just received a report that the airport is still taking fire. The two North Vietnamese platoons are still in the cemetery near Tan Son Nhut. The C-119 was shot down over the airport, and the other aircraft elsewhere. We also understand the C-130s are still on the way but are not landing."

SECRETARY OF DEFENSE SCHLESINGER: "The North Vietnamese have 4,000 sappers in Saigon. They will hit the Embassy if we attack by fire."

PRESIDENT FORD: "I agree. All should leave. We now have made two decisions: First, today is the last day of Vietnamese evacuation. Second, if we fire, our people will go." ...

SECRETARY OF STATE KISSINGER: "We should not let it out that this is the last day of civilian evacuation." ...

SECRETARY OF DEFENSE SCHLESINGER: "There is one question, Henry, that we need to think about. When it is known at the end of the day that this was the last day, will it not provoke panic against our Embassy?"

SECRETARY OF STATE KISSINGER: "I believe that, as the new government comes in, our obligations are terminated." ...

PRESIDENT FORD: "They are one hour away. Even later today, if the situation deteriorates more rapidly than we think, we can go."

CHAIRMAN OF THE JOINT CHIEFS OF STAFF BROWN: "We are 25 minutes away from a ship to the Embassy. We can go on your orders or Graham Martin's."

SECRETARY OF DEFENSE SCHLESINGER: "There is a chance of a night attack." ...

CHAIRMAN OF THE JOINT CHIEFS OF STAFF BROWN: "We are more ready to get people out at Tan Son Nhut than at the Embassy, since at the latter we need to blow up trees and to clear the parking lot."

PRESIDENT FORD: "We need to see what happens at Tan Son Nhut. Then we have to use the DAO and Embassy lift."

SECRETARY KISSINGER: "If they keep up their attacks, it is because they have decided to bottle us up. We should then get everybody out."

PRESIDENT FORD: "Who executes?"

SECRETARY KISSINGER: "I suggest we draft a message here, clear it with Jim and George and show it to you. We will then send it to Graham Martin. Jim can send the same message to [Admiral] Gayler through his channels. Then everybody should know what we are doing."

The message was sent in the morning of the 29th, which was the evening of the 29th in South Vietnam. Secretary Kissinger had the message sent through a top secret cable to Ambassador Graham Martin at the U.S. Embassy in Saigon:

"(1) The President has met with the National Security Council and has made the following decisions: (a) If the airport is open for fixed-wing operations today, you are to continue the evacuation of high-risk Vietnamese by fixed-wing aircraft. You are also to evacuate by the end of the day all American personnel at Tan Son Nhut, as well as all but bare minimum personnel from the Embassy. (b) While you should not say so, this will be the last—repeat—last day of fixed-wing evacuation from Tan Son Nhut. (c) If the airport is unusable for fixed-wing aircraft or becomes so during the day as a result of enemy fire, you are immediately to resort to helicopter evacuation of all—repeat—all Americans, both from the DAO Compound and from the Embassy Compound. Fighter cap and suppressive fire will be used as necessary in the event of helicopter evacuation. (2) Admiral Gayler will be receiving identical instructions from defense. (3) Warm Regards."

* * *

The morning of Wednesday, April 30, began at a very early hour for all residents, foreign diplomats, and visitors in Saigon. It was 4:00 in the morning when the explosions were heard. To those who turned their radios to the U.S. Embassy's Security Network, they heard the call of "Whiskey Joe" in the U.S. Defense Attaché Office Compound at Tan Son Nhut Airport and Airbase. The call of "Whiskey Joe" meant Tan Son Nhut was under attack.

New evacuation plans were to be discussed at the Embassy at 8:00 a.m., but 15 minutes before the meeting U.S. Ambassador Graham Martin left the Embassy to evaluate the damage to Tan Son Nhut Airport. Recognizing the futility of using Tan Son Nhut for any evacuation, he ordered, with the acceptance of Secretary Kissinger, a contingency known as "Operation Frequent Wind" helicopter evacuation from the Embassy.

The streets of Saigon were filled with people scurrying in all directions by motorbike and by foot, some with bags and luggage and roped-together boxes, all this during a disobeyed 24-hour curfew. Outside the U.S. Embassy were throngs of Vietnamese banging on its walls and fences. Streaming from the Embassy's roof were masses of thin straws of paper that were once documents, but now shredded into strings.

Now the American Radio Service repeatedly played what was hardly a secret message anymore: it was those bars of "White Christmas" as a warning to Americans to take action on their previously notified contingencies.

The Embassy staff was leaving from the helipad that topped off a small structure on the rooftop of the Embassy with a 16-foot gray metal stairway leading up to its platform. The Embassy staff was joined on that almost ladder-like 18-stepped stairway by frightened, frantic Vietnamese en mass who wanted to get out with them. One helicopter after another landed to take them off to safety from that helipad, and the helicopters poured their human cargo on the U.S.S. *Blue Ridge* off the coast of the South China Sea.

Soon the quantity of helicopters became unmanageable on the deck of the ship, and after evacuating the escapees, one empty helicopter after another was dumped at sea immediately to make room for the latest incoming ones.

But all of South Vietnam couldn't fit on them, and on that day the phenomenon of the Boat People began: Vietnamese on the seas, searching for refuge.

Hours after the Americans had evacuated South Vietnam, CBS telecast a two and a half hour special entitled *Vietnam: A War That Is Finished*, in which a chronology of American involvement was shown, tracing that American involvement through five U.S. Presidents, surprisingly starting with Truman, then on to Eisenhower, Johnson, Nixon, and Ford. A President was missing from the chronology of Presidents: President Kennedy.

There was also an important sequence missing: films of returned prisoners of war arriving at Clark Air Force Base. Nor was there any other sequence of those returned prisoners praising the United States commitment to South Vietnam. Nor were there any interviews of former prisoners telling of North Vietnamese and Viet Cong tortures they underwent [quoted in Chapter Ten]. There was, however, a rerun of a North Vietnamese propaganda film of "well-treated" American prisoners.

There was a line missing: Charles Collingwood told the audience that after the 1954 Geneva Accords were signed, establishing the 17th parallel as the temporary division be-tween North Vietnam and South Vietnam, the agreements were not supported by either side; a retrospect that should have included the fact that no South Vietnamese had crossed the 17th parallel to invade the North during the entire 21 years from the time the Geneva Accords were signed to the surrender of Saigon on the evening of the telecast.

There were tens of thousands of amputees missing: Two young girls were chosen as the basis for a sequence illustrating the plight of amputees from the war. Of the 80,000 South Vietnamese amputees, the two selected by CBS had lost their limbs not because of the action of the North Vietnamese or Viet Cong, but because of the mistaken firing of South Vietnamese soldiers.

Within the special, John Laurence reported: "The beginning of the end of American involvement became evident in the spring of 1970 as the gears of the Vietnam death machine were grinding more slowly. Four thousand Americans were to die that year, many more Vietnamese, and for the first time, Cambodians. Then days after promising to withdraw another 150,000 American troops from Vietnam, President Nixon on his own authority and without advice or consent of Congress decided to widen the war. It was time, he said, to take action and to clean out the communist sanctuaries in Cambodia. He gave his generals the authority to do what they wanted, to send some 31,000 American soldiers across the border in a final and fateful assault into Cambodia.

"Huge quantities of arms and ammunition, mostly outdated or obsolete, were captured. But the retreating North Vietnamese and Viet Cong carried the war deep into Cambodia and laid the foundations for the successful struggle of the Khmer Rouge.

"The intervention in Cambodia triggered sharp and strenuous protest in the United States, mainly at hundreds of college campuses, most notably at Kent State University. National Guardsmen senselessly opened fire into a crowd of demonstrators, killing four students and wounding nine."

Walter Cronkite was shown saying, "We, the American people, the world's most admired democracy, cannot ever again allow ourselves to be misinformed, manipulated, and misled into disastrous foreign adventures..."

Within *Vietnam: A War That Is Finished*, the Americans to emerge as heroes during the period of U.S. involvement were those members of the news staff of CBS, with some praise also given to other journalists. Throughout the show CBS applauded itself, and as the program drew to a close there was a rolling title that gave screen credit to all those employees of CBS who had brought the war to American living rooms. It was an unparalleled self-tribute, particularly in view of the way the war was ending. Or perhaps that was the point.

The morning after the evacuation of the embassy staff, South Vietnam's President Minh announced the nation's unconditional surrender. A tank smashed down the gates of the Presidential Palace, and South Vietnam as an independent nation was no more.

NBC's Jack Perkins watched Saigon's War Memorial being toppled into the street by North Vietnamese soldiers, and he said to his American television audience that the statue had been "an excess of what money and bad taste accomplish. I don't know if you call it the fall of Saigon or the liberation of Saigon."

Peter Kalisher of CBS said to his American television audience, "For better or worse, the war is over, and how could it be for worse?"

Dinh Ba Thi, the representative of North Vietnam in Paris, expressed his "warm thanks to all socialist countries of national independence and all peace and justice-loving peoples, including the American people who have supported and helped our people in its just struggle. The victory gained today is also theirs."

Walter Cronkite of CBS was asked if he thought television could have changed the course of the war in Indochina if it had reported the war differently. He answered:

"Well, if it had not reported the war, perhaps. If it had failed to do its job, it might have had an effect on the war in Indochina. The fact that the American people saw the horror of war, night after night; lived the frustration of our policy in Vietnam through visual representation of what was happening out there, night after night, must have had an effect. I don't see how it could have failed to. This was what upset the administrations of both Lyndon Johnson and Richard Nixon so much, was that the public was let in on the secret of what war is really like and what we were doing out there. It was impossible for them to carry on a foreign military policy behind the curtain of remoteness which wars of the past permitted."

Which ones? Like World War II?

Saigon's name was changed to Ho Chi Minh City. In a short time the American Embassy was ransacked and left in ruins. Estimates of up to one million residents of what was Saigon were moved to the countryside. "Reeducation camps" were established to hold hundreds of thousands of what were called "undesirable elements." Hard labor, torture, solitary confinement, and executions were common, as were other means of government-sanctioned death. In the cities, typewriters were outlawed; all residents were required to submit to the authorities a list of books they owned, and all residents were required to report "all private conversations deemed contrary to the spirit of the revolution."

The night of the surrender of South Vietnam to North Vietnam, former Senator J. William Fulbright announced that he was "no more depressed than I would be about Arkansas losing a football game to Texas."

4

MAY DAY

THE FIRST DAY of May, 1975, was May Day in every respect: It had been known as a longtime annual holiday in Communist nations, also the signal of an emergency message of distress and danger, and this time it was the first full day since the surrender of South Vietnam. Additionally, on this May Day, a debate that had gone on for weeks in the Congress was belatedly reaching its conclusion in the House of Representatives. It was a bill to permit the use of U.S. troops in the final evacuation from South Vietnam. Since at this stage all U.S. personnel had already been evacuated, it was a vote for or against the U.S. military continuing to evacuate South Vietnamese nationals, including those who had been affiliated with the United States. [The U.S. Senate had previously approved the bill, but both Houses are needed for passage.] Congressman Phil Burton said that using U.S. troops to evacuate Vietnamese would be "a mindless act. Let us reject it." They did. The House of Representatives voted 162 for the bill and 246 against it.

In the issue of *Newsweek* that appeared after the fall of Saigon, a photographic history of that war was presented in an eight-page gallery. There was no photograph of the discovered mass graves of the Hue massacre committed by the North Vietnamese and Viet Cong in which 2,750 bodies were found. Not a single photograph was reprinted of *any* victim from Communist aggression during the entire conflict. Among the photos presented were (*Newsweek*'s captions): "Police chief Loan executes Viet Cong, 1968." "Marine burns hut, 1965." "Victims of My Lai massacre, 1968." "GIs with Saigon whore, 1969." "National Guardsmen fire into a crowd of students at Kent State, 1970." "Outside the Pentagon, antiwar demonstrators spike the guns of military police with flowers, 1967." "ARVN soldier retreats from Laos, 1971." "South Vietnamese prisoner in 'tiger cage,' 1970." "North Vietnamese capture U.S. pilot, 1972." "American army deserter in Sweden, 1968." "B-52 'Stratofortress' rains bombs on North Vietnam during renewed U.S. air strikes at Christmas, 1972." "North Vietnamese hospital, 1968." "Screaming with pain, children flee misdirected napalm attack, 1972."

Time magazine stated within a news story: "Responding as he felt he had to, Ford has nonetheless bobbled his first grand opportunity to lead the nation out of its concentration on a lost cause and to heal the wounds of domestic partisanship over Vietnam. To be sure, he could not with a mere speech assuage the agony or the guilt that many Americans feel when they think of the lost and mined lives, or watch the suffering of the war victims on their television screens. The worry over what still lies ahead for those in Indochina, both Americans and those to whom the U.S. owes a moral debt of gratitude, is real enough. But something more could properly have been expected of a new President who had no need to feel fettered by the mistakes and the policies of the past."

ABC's Harry Reasoner said that "it is now clear that we never should have been involved in Vietnam."

Bui Tin, the Colonel of the North Vietnamese Army who demanded and received the unconditional surrender of South Vietnam on April 30, later talked about the war and said, "Every day our leadership would listen to world news over the radio at 9:00 a.m. to follow the growth of the American anti-war movement. Visits to Hanoi by people like [a movie actress] Jane Fonda and former Attorney General Ramsey Clark and ministers gave us confidence that we should hold on in the face of battlefield reverses. We were elated when Jane Fonda, wearing a red Vietnamese dress, said at a press conference that she was ashamed of American actions in the war and that she would struggle along with us."

Shortly after the fall of Cambodia and South Vietnam, former President Nixon was privately asked what he would have done had he still been president at the time of the imminent surrender of Cambodia and South Vietnam while the 94th Congress rejected all aid to save them. He answered, "I would have bombed the blazes out of Hanoi and Haiphong." Then he added, "Since the Congress hadn't appropriated any funds, I would have probably been impeached for giving the military such an order, but so what? I would have saved thousands—no—let me correct that; millions of Southeast Asian lives."

The former President also referred to the 1936 Supreme Court decision regarding executive versus legislative authority in foreign affairs. [See Chapter Eleven.]

There was more. "And it goes without saying that that action would have preserved international faith in the word of the United States. It doesn't make any difference if it's our word to Thieu or Ton Duc Thang, as you know. Or if it's d'Estang or Brezhnev. Or if it's Harold Wilson or Pol Pot. And so forth. They all have to know we mean what we say. All of them."

When discussing Cambodia, he said that renewed bombing of North Vietnam would have likely discouraged the People's Republic of China's aid to the Khmer Rouge and the Khmer Rouge's aggression against the government of Cambodia— "and if not, Khmer Rouge enclaves would not have been excluded from our bombing. Frankly, knowing what we know now, I should never have stopped it, Congress or no Congress, until all the enclaves were out of business."

U.S. Colonel William E. Legro, who organized Saigon's Intelligence Branch Office and was Advisor to the Army of South Vietnam's Director of Training said, "I felt that the United States, particularly the Congress because they were making the policy, had betrayed the trust that the United States had given South Vietnam. And since I represented the United States, I also felt that I was personally betrayed; I had also made implied promises that the United States would honor the agreements we made at the time of the cease fire, and then when things got really tough we really just cut and run."

* * *

General Van Tien Dung of North Vietnam would later write in his memoirs that because of the cutoff of U.S. aid, President Thieu, the President of South Vietnam, was finally forced to "fight a poor man's war."

There was a further statement from North Vietnam's Colonel Bui Tin: "When Nixon stepped down because of Watergate we knew we would win. Pham Van Dong [Prime Minister of North Vietnam] said of President Ford that 'he's the weakest president in U.S. history. The people didn't elect him. Even if you gave him candy, he doesn't dare to intervene in Vietnam again.' We tested Ford's resolve by attacking Phuoc Long in January, 1975. When Ford kept American B-52s in their hangers, our leadership decided on a big offensive against South Vietnam."

Secretary Kissinger said that if he had any inkling that U.S. aid to American allies would be cut back, "I could not in good conscience have negotiated" the Paris Peace Accords.

Ironically, now exhibited at the Gerald R. Ford Presidential Museum in Grand Rapids, Michigan, is the staircase that led to the helipad on the rooftop of the U.S. Embassy in Saigon onto which Americans and Vietnamese stormed to get out of Saigon.

At President Ford's request, Secretary Kissinger wrote an Eyes Only memorandum for the President, titled "Lessons of Vietnam." Secretary Kissinger wrote, "If one could offer any guidelines for the future about the lessons to be drawn regarding domestic support for foreign policy, it would be that political groups will not long remain comfortable in positions that go against their traditional attitudes. The liberal Democrats could not long support a war against a revolutionary movement, no matter how reactionary the domestic tactics of that movement. They had accepted the heavy commitment because of President Kennedy, whom they regarded as their leader, but they withdrew from it under President Johnson.

"Our diplomacy also suffered in the process, and it may take us some time to bring things back to balance. We often found that the United States could not sustain a diplomatic position for more than a few weeks or months before it came under attack from the same political elements that had often advocated that very position. We ended up negotiating with ourselves, constantly offering concession after concession while the North Vietnamese changed nothing in their diplomatic objectives and very little in their diplomatic positions. It was only in secret diplomacy that we could hold anything approaching a genuine dialogue, and even then the North Vietnamese could keep us under constant pressure. Our diplomacy often degenerated into frantic efforts to find formulas that would evoke momentary support and would gloss over obvious differences between ourselves and the North Vietnamese. The legacy of this remains to haunt us, making it difficult for us to sustain a diplomatic position for any length of time, no matter how obdurate the enemy, without becoming subject to domestic attack."

The April 1975 surrenders did not conclude the posting of white flags in Southeast Asia. In seven months the domino principle took another casualty: Laos, overseen by 30,000 Vietnamese troops. On December 2, 1975 the nation's name was changed to the Lao People's Democratic Republic. Although 200,000 Laotians managed to escape to Thailand, Laos soon had more political prisoners per capita than any other country in the world, including North Vietnam and Cambodia. Laos followed the pattern established by North Vietnam by sending "the undesirables" who hadn't managed to escape, to "reeducation camps." Some "undesirables" became used by both Soviets and North Vietnamese for experimentation with poison gas. It soon became known among Laotians that to be transported to Phou Fa mountain of Phongsali Province in northern Laos [Phongsali sometimes spelled Phong Saly] meant never to be heard from again. Former King Savang Vatthana was reported to have been starved to death in an unnamed detention camp. [Some reports said he died in May of 1979, others as late as 1981.] In addition, there soon came the slaughter of the Hmong people of Laos.

The peace in Southeast Asia which demonstrators demanded and our 94th Congress enacted caused millions of deaths. More were killed in just the first year of peace than during the preceding decade of war.

After the defeat of Cambodia and South Vietnam, a leading network newscaster was privately asked why he and his network were not reporting the genocide that was going on in Cambodia. His answer was that "there is no way to bring cameramen in there. Television is a visual medium and we need pictures."

The man who questioned him then responded, "But when there is a courtroom drama and you are not allowed to bring in cameras, you hire an illustrator to draw the scene in the courtroom. In this case, you could even get *live* witnesses on camera; not drawings but real people. While you have brave investigative reporters finding out and revealing C.I.A. secrets to the public, they seem to have such difficulty interviewing a Cambodian refugee when Thailand border areas have 34,000 Cambodian escapees there right now."

The network newscaster looked down, then back up, and had no response other than a small shrug.

The three networks had consistent shrugs for the genocide. There seemed to be no other reason for their refusal to inform the American public other than they had been false prophets, disregarding those who warned of a coming bloodbath.

With little exception, what brought the story to the American people didn't come until 1978, when NBC ran a television miniseries [in four parts from April the 16th to the 19th of 1978] titled *Holocaust*, regarding the Nazi-committed holocaust of World War II. Within a week of the series [April the 25th], Bill Safire wrote a *New York Times* column comparing the events of Cambodia with the Nazi holocaust, and Jack Anderson had similar observations in his *Washington Post* column the next week [May the 2nd]. Normally those two columnists had opposing political views, but in their revelations regarding Cambodia, their conclusions superseded their usual differences.

Jack Anderson said he had a "two-inch stack of refugee accounts, verified photos and medical records, also access to confidential documents and analyses from the State Department, Justice Department, C.I.A. and the White House."

It was not until after the Safire and Anderson columns were written and printed that there were significant stories by the *Washington Post*, the *New York Times*, and on television by David Brinkley, and statements from President Carter and Senator McGovern, who now condemned the Khmer Rouge of Cambodia, some three years too late.

A frequent excuse was given that what had happened in Cambodia during those three years was unknown at the time, while others said what had happened there was classified during those years. There was not one shred of truth to either of those statements. But worse among them were those who had previously predicted that Pol Pot's Khmer Rouge would not create a bloodbath, and after the bloodbath they changed their stories by saying that *Americans* created the Khmer Rouge's bloodbath as the Khmer Rouge's reaction to previous U.S. bombing raids in Cambodia. That wasn't just a corruption of history; it was a corruption of logic. It would make as much sense to say that the horrors committed by the Nazis were the fault of U.S. bombers.

All the consequences and excuses could so easily have been avoided. All that had to be done was for the 94th U.S. Congress to accept the victory achieved by the United States and the non-Communist governments of South Vietnam and Cambodia. It is all very simple: the majority of the 94th Congress did not want to do that.

5

JOURNEYS FROM NATIONS GONE

ALTHOUGH BOAT PEOPLE became a phenomenon, the uniqueness was not because Vietnamese were risking their lives to seek freedom. They had been doing that by the millions who journeyed from North Vietnam to South Vietnam since 1954 when the 17th parallel was designated as the line between the two Vietnams. The uniqueness of the Boat People was that now with the fall of South Vietnam as well as neighboring Cambodia, and an inhospitable falling Laos, the safest exit from Communist rule appeared to be the sea.

The Boat People went to whatever land would come in sight from their rafts and from other unseaworthy vessels hardly worthy of being called vessels, some nothing more than pieces of wood tied together with ropes. Estimates numbered them at one million starting the journey, but only some 500,000 completing it, with the other half of them under the South China Sea to this day. Some of them (number unknown) were Vietnamese who were ethnic Chinese and were not willing Boat People but were forced onto rafts by the new government in Ho Chi Minh City, so as to be done with them due to their heritage.

The Boat People were subject not only to the sea, but to death by thirst and starvation and the diseases that come from squalor—and from takeover by pirates from Thailand and other Southeast Asian nations who plundered, raped, murdered, and even cannibalized their captives at sea.

Most survivors who made it to land arrived in Asian refugee centers of Hong Kong, Malaysia, Singapore, Thailand, Indonesia, the Philippines, Japan, and Australia. Of all of them, Great Britain's Crown Colony of Hong Kong took more Boat People in and also afforded the best accommodations; crowded but still the best for many years. At Hong Kong's Jubilee Refugee Center, each barracks-style building housed thirty-two in three tiers of beds, with refugees spending daytime outside the barracks in the center's recreation areas and streets. As with the other Asian refugee centers, Hong Kong was not meant to be a final destination of the Boat People but rather a "First Asylum," and all refugees knew it was a temporary stop on the way to somewhere that was yet to be designated. The place of final destination most often wanted by the Boat People was the United States. They quickly learned of the debate in the U.S. Congress as to whether or not the United States should accept them. And they just as quickly learned what some of the most prominent members of the U.S. Congress were saying publicly: Senator George McGovern said, "Ninety percent of the Vietnamese refugees would be better off going back to their own land." California

Congressman Burt Talcott said, "Damn it, we have too many Orientals already!" Senator Robert Byrd said, "I think some of these people should be sent back." Senator Richard Clark gave a reason beyond prejudice for rejecting Vietnamese, saying, "it would hamper the possibility of negotiations with Hanoi," as though, at that point, there was anything to negotiate, or that any U.S. negotiation would be successful.

In the end, humanity won the debate and the United States accepted hundreds of thousands of Southeast Asian refugees; six times more than any other single nation. In total, including Boat People from Vietnam, land refugees from Cambodia, and a scattered amount from Laos, the total reached 800,000.

Learning the English language became their highest priority and was generally their first accomplishment. Ninety-five percent of the new U.S. residents became employed. It is impossible to accurately give statistics measuring their benefit to the United States but, beyond argument, it was huge and no one can accurately state they were a burden. [Non-Asian nations that accepted Vietnamese Boat People in smaller but significant amounts were Canada, France, Germany, United Kingdom, Israel, Italy, and Belgium.]

Many Boat People went to camps and holding centers in Thailand and Malaysia, which were meant to be even more temporary than the refugee centers in other Asian nations. For most of those who found refuge in the camps of Thailand and Malaysia, it was a new horror.

At Malaysia's Kuala Terengganu's shore line was the site of a refugee holding center where there were thousands and thousands of Vietnamese without shelters or sanitation, but just a vast field of sand from which many Malaysians threw rocks at them, and the rock-throwing was not stopped by authorities. The rock-throwing stopped only when Malaysian naval patrol boats took over and Vietnamese were sent back to the sea.

On Thursday, June the 7th of 1979, Pope John Paul II visited the remains of Poland's Auschwitz Nazi Concentration Camp and said, "It is necessary to think with fear of how far cruelty can go." It was not a controversial statement; only an accurate and humane statement. But he didn't influence everyone in the world.

The morning after the Pope's visit, at 6:00 a.m., 110 brightly painted empty busses arrived at Aranyaprathet in Thailand, where refugees from Cambodia and Vietnam were being held. Those refugees were put aboard a caravan of busses at Aranyaprathet. They were not told where they were going, but some had a premonition and they tried to escape the Thai soldiers who were administering the boarding process. Those who tried to escape the imminent journey were clubbed and beaten and forced back into the busses. The soldiers told them they had their orders. The busses headed for the Cambodian border full and came back empty, then were filled up again and headed for the Cambodian border full and came back empty. And again and again the process went on until 43,000 refugees were gone beyond the horizon. That number was reached by the following Monday, four days after the Pope's statement at Auschwitz.

On the following Friday, Malaysia announced that 76,000 refugees were being sent back to sea. The designated destination was arrival in international waters. It was further announced that legislation would be enacted to shoot on sight any Boat People found trying to enter Malaysia.

At the same time, the United States was accepting 7,000 Vietnamese a month. The 96th U.S. Congress was holding up funds for allowing 5,000 more Vietnamese refugees into the United States. It cannot be denied that if they allowed even one of those 5,000 refugees to die, then the Congress was choosing the death of that person over an inconvenience of our own. This was the tragic epitome of the George Santayana's quote: "Those who cannot remember the past are condemned to repeat it." By this time surely most members of the Congress had either read *The Diary of Anne Frank* or seen the play or the movie based on her diary. At least they had heard of Anne Frank and had learned that Anne Frank's life was ended 34 years earlier in the concentration camp of Bergen-Belsen. The Congress did not stop to think that their current action could bring the fate of Anne Frank to someone of their own time: Ahn Pham.

They never heard of her. And besides, the concentration camp called Bergen-Belsen was much easier to pronounce than the "reeducation camp" called Xuan Phuac.

By this time [1979], President Carter became the leading voice for the rescue and acceptance of more Southeast Asian refugees, opposing many members of his own party in the Congress, and he won. At a United Nations conference held in Geneva that July, U.S. Vice President Mondale gave a magnificent speech in support of rescue operations and resettlement of Southeast Asian refugees. Since the United States was doing so much more than any other nation, both in rescue operations and resettlement, his remarks had great credibility.

But there was a flat note in his speech as he echoed what many of the other delegates were advocating—that Vietnam should take more effective steps to halt the numbers of refugees escaping from Vietnam. What was now being advocated was not an international call for Vietnam to end the enslavement, but an international call for Vietnam to increase the guards.

Before the conference was done, the Secretary General of the United Nations, Kurt Waldheim, announced that through its Orderly Departure Program, "The Government of the Socialist Republic of Vietnam has authorized me to inform you that for a reasonable period of time it will make every effort to stop illegal departures."

That statement was too similar to a Saturday night meeting of the Soviet Union's Warsaw Pact in August of 1961. After midnight the conferees heard that over the years, three million East Berliners had left East Berlin to live in West Berlin, and the migration from the east to west was now accelerating at the rate of over 2,000 a day. The Soviet Union announced that it must be stopped. Before Sunday's dawn, construction was started on the Berlin Wall. There followed a great debate in the West as to whether or not the United States should tear down the Wall, or the four allied powers of West Berlin should jointly tear it down, or that it must be left standing since the Wall was being built on property of East Berlin under the jurisdiction of the Soviet Union, and tearing it down by any party of the West could well start World War III. Those were the three choices. No one in the West argued that the Soviet Union should build the Wall *higher*.

* * *

But by 1979 the political culture of those who lived in liberty had vastly changed from 18 years back. Many in this generation were fresh from protesting in the streets, waving flags of North Vietnam and the Viet Cong. Therefore, they did not identify with those Southeast Asians who were escaping from the very governments many of those protesters had publicly favored. Their past dictated that, to them, the Boat People and other escapees from Southeast Asian countries were not friends, but were fools who fought against, or at least did not join, those who wanted to take over their government.

Those in the makeshift boats were giving visual and audible evidence to the entire world that the government that won the war was of such a nature that it was causing South Vietnamese to gamble with death on the high seas, rather than live under the jurisdiction of the new government.

It should be known that there were some wartime protestors who grieved for what had happened. Some of those who were public in their advocacies of anti-U.S. policy during the war were now public in their reassessments.

One of the most notable was David Horowitz, who had been an editor of the most celebrated far-left magazine, *Ramparts*, as well as being a friend and associate of Marxists and Black Panthers. After what happened to Cambodians and Vietnamese from the Communist victories in their countries, David Horowitz made a sharp turn in his political direction and devoted the rest of his life to making up for the damage in which he participated during those years. He became the founder of the David Horowitz Freedom Center.

The sociologist and author Professor Peter L. Berger [Boston University] wrote that he was compelled to face the question of his own earlier thinking, and that "the direction of the refugee streams tells its own story . . . The terror imposed on South Vietnam by its conquerors has been vastly worse than anything perpetrated by the old Saigon regime, both in quantity and quality. There were no Boat People trying to escape from Thieu." He wrote that although he had never been to Southeast Asia, "it was television images that aroused my moral outrage and led me to become a vocal opponent of the Vietnam War . . . It is now clear that, roughly from 1967 on, there was a strong anti-war feeling behind major American reporting from Indochina . . . The consequences of Hanoi's victory have been a human catastrophe of monumental dimensions." And regarding his own experiences in opposition to U.S. policy, "I saw the movement taken over for their own purposes by people who were not interested in stopping the war but in defeating and humiliating America." [Excerpts from his article, "Indochina and the American Conscience," published in *Commentary* magazine, February 1980.]

More recently came the striking example of the Academy Award–winning actor Jon Voight. While many Hollywood celebrities were making public statements that the United States should withdraw from Iraq in the War against Islamic Terrorism without first winning, Jon Voight was dedicating himself to insure that those in the younger generation would not do what he did in his youth during the Southeast Asian War. Through countless public appearances on radio, television, and to private groups, he stated his deepest regret for the views he held in those earlier years. His devotion became a daily cause.

The musician and singer Joan Baez, the world-famous American folk singer, who had been a near-fixture at demonstrations against U.S. policy during the Southeast Asian War, did not seek to reappraise her own activities but felt betrayed by the government of North Vietnam and took out a remarkable ad on May the 30th of 1979. It was titled "Open Letter to the Socialist Republic of Vietnam" in major newspapers throughout the United States. [The *New York Times, Los Angeles Times, San Francisco Examiner, San Francisco Chronicle,* and *Washington Post.*] The publication in those newspapers was paid for by her Humanitarian International Human Rights Committee. The heart of her message was: "We have heard the horror stories from the people of Vietnam—from workers and peasants, Catholic nuns and Buddhist priests, from the Boat People, the artists and professionals and those who fought alongside the N.L.F. The jails are overflowing with thousands upon thousands of 'detainees.' People disappear and never return. People are shipped to 'reeducation centers,' fed a starvation diet of stale rice, forced to squat bound waist to ankle, suffocated in 'connex' boxes. People are used as human mine detectors, clearing live mine fields with their hands and feet. For many, life is hell and death is prayed for."

In asking others to co-sign the ad, one who refused to sign the message was Jane Fonda.

Nearly three decades later, Ted Turner, the founder of Cable News Network (CNN) appeared as a guest on *The O'Reilly Factor* of Fox Network News [December the 9th of 2008]. Bill O'Reilly said to Ted Turner, "I asked Ms. Fonda, [Jane Fonda was the former wife of Ted Turner] 'Didn't it ever bother you that after all your activism and getting America out of Vietnam, which it subsequently did in the mid-70s, that three million human beings were slaughtered by the people that you were lionizing, the North Vietnamese and the Khmer Rouge Communists, who wouldn't have been slaughtered if we'd stayed? And their skulls were stacked on top of one another. And I never heard a word from you, Jane Fonda.' And I never heard a word from Ted Turner about that. And that, to me, is a good question."

Ted Turner answered, "You got me. I didn't really think about it. You know, it didn't make the news very much at the time."

"No, it didn't," Bill O'Reilly sadly agreed.

At least Ted Turner publicly admitted, "I didn't really think about it."

There is no reason to doubt the truth of that statement.

All of this would not be worth writing here if all, or at least most prominent people who had opposed U.S. involvement during the war, took public note of what was happening in the Communist-conquered nations. But they didn't. By the end of the decade of the 1970s the plight of the Boat People from Vietnam was so well known, and the genocide of Cambodia was so well known, and the imprisonment of Laotians was so well known, and yet most of those who were so influential in opposing U.S. policy in Southeast Asia chose the continuation of rejecting the obvious. If their cause of earlier years was truly to save human lives and decry human misery, why did their cause end when the deaths and human misery so massively increased? If they cared enough to save the jurisdiction of totalitarians who were intent on bringing an *end* to liberties, why not protest the death of those who were *seeking* liberty?

Even after the genocidal years began, motion pictures and television docudramas often had themes that justified the stand their makers had taken against U.S. policy during the war. The films did not go forward in time to show the post-war horror, as that would have defeated their earlier self-righteousness. Instead, their new message rested on the premise that those who served in the military and sacrificed in that war were naïvely wrong, and every widow and other bereaved family member who saw the films was meant to feel they should have influenced their loved one to be a draft-dodger, or surely not a volunteer. They seemed to convey the message that those who gave their lives or their limbs were just too unsophisticated to see it the way the Hollywoodians who sacrificed nothing had seen it.

Well into those genocidal years, they did not start production on films or docudramas on the Boat People or the millions of other Southeast Asian victims of surrender. Their records of Southeast Asian events seemed to stop before January of 1973. The prospect of their screenplays going through the time of the Paris Peace Accords and into the surrenders of April 1975 was a Hollywood taboo. The British film *The Killing Fields* was not made until 1984, and even in that film, the *New York Times* journalist who was portrayed in the film, Sidney Schanberg, was made into a hero who, in truth, wrote favorably about the Khmer Rouge during the war years [as quoted in Chapter Two].

The injustice of the calendar-stopping films was that younger people were being told stories that were often brilliantly designed to evoke a political emotion exonerating the advocacies of their filmmakers. As a result, many surviving veterans found themselves still in combat against the same domestic forces who challenged them during the war.

On theater screens and television sets, veterans were treated with sympathy. That sympathy was as cruel as what the filmmakers did to them during the war. The veterans were now portrayed as drug-addicts, alcoholics, and other kinds of misfits or, at best, just sad characters unable to adjust to civilian life; ruined either physically or mentally or both by U.S. policy-makers.

But "The Forgotten Veteran" as one popular television program portrayed him, was, in reality, "The Remembered Veteran," while the real forgotten veterans were the vast majority who came home feeling all the pains of war that any veterans from any war have felt. They did not see themselves as victims, but integrated back into their home cities as self-disciplined, productive, and contributing members of U.S. society; this time without uniform.

The Hollywood dream-makers should have been the ones receiving sympathy, since they had disabilities far greater than the vast majority of war veterans from Southeast Asian battles. The self-love of Hollywoodians made them blind, deaf, and mute to the truth that was all around them.

So many celebrities were such an immense influence on the youth of the times, yet after the Southeast Asian surrenders the youth were not summoned by their mentors to march down Pennsylvania Avenue again, this time to protest what Southeast Asia had become under its conquerors. The youth were not sent leaflets by Benjamin Spock or Daniel Ellsberg or Ramsey Clark or Jane Fonda or Tom Hayden to demonstrate in the streets of their cities so as to bring attention to the genocide of Cambodians and the executions, tortures, and prisons of Vietnam and Laos, nor did they advocate a plan to rescue the Boat

People. By and large, their old cause had been accomplished, and so they went back to formal events, talking about other things while in great part the result of their previous pursuits were ghoulishly spread across the countries of Southeast Asia and buried under the South China Sea.

6

BEFORE PARIS

TO FEEL THE weight of the Post-Paris events, it is helpful to keep in mind the span of U.S. Presidents who gave support to the defense of South Vietnam.

By the end of President Eisenhower's Administration there were 885 U.S. armed forces in South Vietnam. By the end of President Kennedy's Administration the number had increased to 16,300. By the end of President Johnson's Administration there were 536,100. On November the 3rd of 1969, President Nixon announced the beginning of what he called "Vietnamization," which was a plan for the South Vietnamese to be trained and incrementally take the place of U.S. ground combatants. By the end of 1972, one month before the signing of the Paris Peace Accords, U.S. Armed Forces had been reduced by 506,100 to a total of 24,200.

* * *

Years back [April 7, 1954], President Eisenhower first used the term *domino principle* in explaining his sending of military advisors to South Vietnam. In response to a question asked by Robert Richards of the Copley Press regarding the importance of Indochina to the free world, President Eisenhower responded, ". . . You have the possibility that many human beings pass under a dictatorship that is inimical to the free world. Finally, you have broader considerations that might follow what you would call the falling domino principle. You have a row of dominos set up; you knock over the first one, and what will happen to the last one is the certainty that it will go over quickly. So you could have a beginning of a disintegration that would have the most profound influences."

Months later [October 23, 1954], President Eisenhower sent a message to Ngo Dinh Diem, Premier of South Vietnam, in which he wrote, "Your recent requests for aid to assist in the formidable project of the movement of several hundred thousand loyal Vietnam citizens away from areas [North Vietnam] which are passing under a de facto rule and political ideology which they abhor, are being fulfilled." Years later he said to President Diem [May 9, 1957], "The cost of defending freedom, of defending America, must be paid in many forms and in many places . . . Military as well as economic help is currently needed in Vietnam."

In the second year of President Kennedy's Administration [February 5, 1962], President Kennedy sent a message to the people of South Vietnam on the occasion of their annual Tet observance of the beginning of the Lunar New Year, celebrating the incoming Year of the Tiger: "In your struggle against the aggressive forces of Communism, the sacrifices that you have willingly made, the courage you have shown, the burdens you have endured, have been a source of inspiration to people all over the world. Let me assure you of our continued assistance in the development of your capabilities to maintain your freedom and to defeat those who wish to destroy that freedom. We in America sincerely hope that the Year of the Tiger will see peace come again to Vietnam. We know that courage and dedication to peace and freedom will prevail and that prospects for Vietnam will brighten during the coming year. And we look confidently with you to the day when your country will again be at peace—united, prosperous, and free."

At the President's News Conference of September the 12th, 1963, less than three months before his assassination, President Kennedy said: "What helps to win the war, we support; what interferes with the war effort, we oppose . . . We want the war to be won, the communists to be contained, and the Americans to go home. That is our policy. I am sure it is the policy of the people of South Vietnam. But we are not there to see a war lost, and we will follow the policy which I have indicated today of advancing those causes and issues which help win the war."

President Kennedy was, of course, assassinated in Dallas on November the 22nd of 1963, as his motorcade drove toward the Trade Mart for a luncheon where the President was prepared to speak on national security. Barely mentioned is that within his prepared text were the following excerpts: "If we are strong, our words will speak for themselves. If we are weak, words will be of no help. I realize that this nation often tends to identify turning-points in world affairs with the major addresses that preceded them. But it was not the Monroe Doctrine that kept all Europe away from this hemisphere—it was the strength of the British fleet and the width of the Atlantic Ocean. It was not General Marshall's speech at Harvard which kept Communism out of Western Europe—it was the strength and stability made possible by our military and economic assistance. In this administration also it has been necessary at times to issue specific warnings—warnings that we could not stand by and watch the Communists conquer Laos by force, or intervene in the Congo, or swallow West Berlin, or maintain offensive missiles on Cuba. But while our goals were at least temporarily obtained in these and other instances, our successful defense of freedom was due not to the words we used, but with the strength we stood ready to use on behalf of the principles we stand ready to defend . . .

"Our security and strength, in the last analysis, directly depend on the security and strength of others, and that is why our military and economic assistance plays such a key role in enabling those who live on the periphery of the Communist world to maintain their independence of choice. Our assistance to these nations can be painful, risky and costly, as is true in Southeast Asia today. But we dare not weary of the task."

President Johnson, at a News Conference [August 6, 1965], said: "If we are driven from the field in Vietnam, then no nation can ever again have the same confidence in American promise or in American protection. We are in Vietnam to fulfill one of the most solemn pledges of the American nation. Three Presidents—President Eisenhower, President Kennedy and your present President—over eleven years have committed themselves and have promised to help defend this small and valiant nation. Strengthened by that promise, the people of South Vietnam have fought for many long years. Thousands of them have died. Thousands more have been crippled and scarred by war. And we just cannot now dishonor our word, or abandon our commitment, or leave those who believed us and who trusted us to the terror and repression and murder that would follow."

Twelve days later [August 18, 1965], former President Eisenhower phoned President Johnson about Vietnam, saying, "Now, if you look up my record I constantly said, we are going to support Vietnam." This was in reference to his actions in relation to the April 27, 1954 Geneva Accords that had split Vietnam into North and South. "We didn't sign the treaty but all the rest of the nations did except South Vietnam and ourselves. That treaty had certain measures that precluded real military positioning of troops there except the term's advisors, and we did that. Now, when I left [the presidency], when I was in my last year there, we had about 365 advisors and I think we'd run it up to about 600 because of the size of the country. But I did say constantly, 'We are going to support Vietnam.'" Then, in relation to President Johnson's Vietnam policy, former President Eisenhower said, "Now, I've constantly said in the condition that it is today, I support the President consistently and fully."

President Johnson responded, "I know that."

Toward the end of the conversation, when talking about the difficulties with the U.S. press, former President Eisenhower offered, "Well, as I say, pay no attention to those darn people." [Lyndon Baines Johnson Presidential Library]

The Year of the Monkey began on Tuesday, January the 30th of 1968, in what became the last full year of the Johnson

Administration. This particular Tet holiday is known as the day the opinion of many Americans took a change from supporting U.S. policy toward South Vietnam to opposition of that policy. That accurate assessment is part of the amnesia that haunts the history of the war.

The Tet offensive of North Vietnam and the Viet Cong was planned to bring about the quick and total defeat of South Vietnam during a 36-hour truce for the holiday of the Lunar New Year. It was planned to come about through coordinated and simultaneous attacks against more than 100 cities of South Vietnam, including the takeover of the capital city of Saigon. They, indeed, attacked most large cities and many small ones, but only succeeded in taking over the city of Hue in the far north of South Vietnam. In totality, it was a military disaster for North Vietnam and the Viet Cong, in which their combatants suffered immense casualties and the ruin of their most valuable military assets. The White House and the Department of Defense were exchanging congratulations over the enemy's defeat in its Tet offensive. But it was not the way the major media reacted. Within hours, the North Vietnamese and the Viet Cong enjoyed a major psychological victory due to the reporting by much of the U.S. media.

As in most foreign capital cities, the symbol of the United States was the U.S. Embassy. In the case of Saigon, the U.S. Embassy was on four acres of mid-city property with a fortified chancery building of six stories topped with a smaller two-story structure topped by a helicopter pad on its summit. On January the 31st, during the Tet offensive, NBC Television reported that 20 suicide commandos were reported to be holding the first floor of the embassy, while the Associated Press reported that Viet Cong suicide commandos were holed up in the building.

The *Washington Post* wrote, "Guerrillas seized part of the building and held it against attacking American military policemen and paratroops."

The Associated Press reported, "The Viet Cong seized part of the United States Embassy in Saigon early Wednesday, Vietnam time. Snipers are on buildings and on rooftops near the embassy and are firing on American personnel inside the compound. Twenty suicide commandos are reported to be holding the first floor of the embassy." This, accompanied by other similar reports, was used in media throughout the world.

Dramatic, but not accurate. Not one potential invader was successful in getting in any building of the U.S. Embassy Compound. One member of the Viet Cong was shot and killed on the lawn of the grounds, which indicated that he climbed the eight-foot wall off Thong Nhat Street and got into the compound grounds, but was killed before getting inside the chancery or any building of the U.S. Embassy.

Perhaps more influential than anyone during this period was Walter Cronkite of CBS, who told his audience, "Early Wednesday, Vietnam time, the Communists struck at the heart of Saigon and seized part of the new American Embassy. At dawn, American military police tried to storm into the Embassy but were driven back by the Viet Cong force, estimated at twenty men. The Communist suicide squad held part of the first floor."

Throughout the war it was commonly said by opponents of U.S. policy that the war was nothing other than a civil war between the Viet Cong of South Vietnam and the South Vietnamese Government. (As referred to earlier, the Viet Cong was also known as the National Liberation Front for the Liberation of South Vietnam, the N.L.F., the Provisional Revolutionary Government, and the P.R.G.) Supporters of U.S. policy argued that the Viet Cong served under the direction of North Vietnam, and the war was not a South Vietnamese civil war. After the surrender of South Vietnam, North Vietnam's Colonel Bui Tin [the recipient of South Vietnam's surrender], was asked by Stephen Young, a human-rights activist, "Was the National Liberation Front an independent movement of Vietnam?"

Bui Tin answered, "No. It was set up by our Communist Party to implement a decision of the Third Party Congress of September 1960. We always said there was only one party, only one army in the war to liberate the South and unify the nation. At all times there was only one party commissar in command of the South." The U.S. Government did not need or receive that confirmation during the war since the White House and the Department of Defense knew the line of command, including North Vietnam's direction of the Tet offensive, but Bui Tin's late confirmation could at least be helpful to historians. But, realistically, most likely it won't be.

Against the background of the 1968 Tet Offensive came the campaign for the Presidency of the United States. It has now become "history" that during that campaign, candidate Nixon told the nation that he had "a secret plan to end the war in Vietnam." The only problem with that insertion into history is that he didn't say that. When, in later years, he talked about the story, he smiled and said, "If I had a secret plan to end the war it wouldn't have been secret for long, because the first thing I would have done is tell Lyndon what the secret plan was. During the campaign, when I was quoted as saying that, I answered publicly that if I had a gimmick, a magic formula, I'd tell L.B.J. I don't think anyone other than the wire services repeated what I said" [a reference to the Associated Press of May the 14th, 1968]. As of the time of the writing of this book no one has yet come up with a time and place such a statement of a secret plan was made. But "history" with quotation marks became history without quotation marks, and so most of the current generations have been told fiction.

A danger that continued to face the U.S. and South Vietnamese troops were the sanctuaries used by the North Vietnamese military and the Viet Cong inside neighboring Cambodia. North Vietnam and the Viet Cong had taken over part of the territory, pushing all Cambodians out and stocking areas with its own military as well as thousands of tons of armaments. After the North Vietnamese and Viet Cong stationed there attacked South Vietnam, they would flee back to safety in what were known as privileged sanctuaries in Cambodia.

Cambodia's Head of State, Prince Norodom Sihanouk, had earlier [January 10, 1968] told Chester Bowles, a representative of President Johnson, that "we don't want any Vietnamese in Cambodia. We will be very glad if you solve our problem. We are not opposed to hot pursuit in uninhabited areas. You will liberate us from the Viet Cong. For me, only Cambodia counts. I want you to force the Viet Cong to leave Cambodia." The difficulty was that if the United States was to do as he wanted, and if the United States made it public, Prince Sihanouk could no longer claim his country was neutral, which was a perception he wanted to maintain, particularly by the People's Republic of China, who could turn against him. Therefore President Nixon, in his first year in office, made the decision to bomb the heretofore privileged sanctuaries without public exposure. He did, however, tell and received the approval of the Chairman of the Senate Armed Services Committee, Senator Richard Russell, and the committee's Ranking Member, Senator John Stennis.

Even with so few Americans informed, the information was revealed in the nation's press and became known as "The Secret Bombing of Cambodia." Prince Sihanouk held a news conference [May 13, 1969] in which it became obvious that he approved of the bombing but wanted to retain his public neutrality. He said, "Here it is, the first report about several B-52 bombings. Yet I have not been informed about that at all because I have not lost any houses, any countrymen, nothing, nothing. Nobody was caught in those barrages. Nobody. No Cambodians. If there is a buffalo or any Cambodian killed, I will be informed immediately. But this is an affair between the Americans and the Viet Cong-Viet Minh without any Khmer [Cambodian] witnesses. There have been no Khmer witnesses, so how can I protest?" At a later press conference he added that Hanoi had crowded so many communist troops into that area of Cambodia that it was "practically North Vietnamese territory." Prince Sihanouk then invited President Nixon to visit him in Phnom Penh.

In President Nixon's major address of November the 3rd, 1969, along with his announcement of his plan for Vietnamization, he added a chronology of consistency of prior presidential policy that he would not violate: "In response to the request of the Government of South Vietnam, President Eisenhower sent economic aid and military equipment to assist the people of South Vietnam in their efforts to prevent a Communist takeover. Seven years ago, President Kennedy sent 16,000 military personnel to Vietnam as combat advisers. Four years ago, President Johnson sent American combat forces to South Vietnam . . .

"Three American Presidents have recognized the great stakes involved in Vietnam and understood what had to be done. In 1963, President Kennedy, with his characteristic eloquence and clarity, said: 'We want to see a stable government there, carrying on a struggle to maintain its national independence. We believe strongly in that. We are not going to withdraw from that effort. In my opinion, for us to withdraw from that effort would mean a collapse not only of South Vietnam, but Southeast Asia. So we are going to stay there.'

"President Eisenhower and President Johnson expressed the same conclusion during their terms of office. For the future of peace, precipitate withdrawal would thus be a disaster of immense magnitude. A nation cannot remain great if it betrays its allies and lets down its friends. Our defeat and humiliation in South Vietnam without question would promote recklessness in the councils of those great powers who have not yet abandoned their goals of world conquest . . .

"In San Francisco a few weeks ago, I saw demonstrators carrying signs reading: 'Lose in Vietnam, bring the boys home.' Well, one of the strengths of our free society is that any American has a right to reach that conclusion and to advocate that point of view. But as President of the United States, I would be untrue to my oath of office if I allowed the policy of this Nation to be dictated by the minority who hold that point of view and who try to impose it on the Nation by mounting demonstrations in the street . . . Let historians not record that when America was the most powerful nation in the world we passed on the other side of the road and allowed the last hopes for peace and freedom of millions of people to be suffocated by the forces of totalitarianism. And so tonight—to you, the great silent majority of my fellow Americans—I ask for your support . . .

"Let us be united for peace. Let us also be united against defeat. Because let us understand: North Vietnam cannot defeat or humiliate the United States. Only Americans can do that."

His warning was prophetic because only Americans *could* do and *did* do that. Some Americans were taking part in marches of protest that would bring defeat and humiliation for the United States—and would cause the people of Cambodia and South Vietnam the loss of their nations and the loss of millions of lives.

7

HO! HO! HO CHI MINH!
THE N.L.F. IS GOING TO WIN!

WITH PRESIDENT JOHNSON out of office and President Nixon in office for almost ten months, the old chants of "Hey! Hey! L.B.J.! How Many Kids Did You Kill Today?" were replaced with the chant: "Ho! Ho! Ho Chih Minh! The N.L.F. is Going to Win!"

Looking east on Pennsylvania Avenue came the sight of over 200,000 protestors marching from the Capitol grounds in the direction of the White House [October the 15th, 1969]. They were yelling the chants mixed with profanities and cheers, with its leaders yelling questions: "What do we want?" and those behind them in the march shouting back, "Peace!" Then the leaders yelled, "When do we want it?" and those behind them shouted back, "Now!" Some held dowel sticks high with the flag of North Vietnam or the flag of the Viet Cong attached to the sticks. There were others who waved American flags, but those were hoisted upside-down.

Just days prior to the demonstration, North Vietnam Premier Pham Van Dong had broadcast on Radio Hanoi with the salutation, "To my dear American friends."

"This fall, large sectors of the U.S. people, encouraged and supported by many peace- and justice-loving American personages, are launching a broad and powerful offensive throughout the United States to demand that the Nixon Administration put an end to the Vietnam aggressive war, and immediately bring all American troops home. We are firmly confident that with the solidarity and bravery of the peoples of our two countries and with the approval and support of peace-loving people in the world, the struggle of the Vietnamese people and U.S. progressive people against U.S. aggression will certainly be crowned with total victory. May your fall offensive succeed splendidly."

It did succeed as splendidly as planned, and another demonstration was held one month later, on November the 15th, for an even more splendid success.

November's 15th would be a Saturday going into Sunday morning, in contrast to the Wednesday of the previous one in October; the weekend offering easier availability to those who couldn't come in mid-week. It began in the dark of Saturday's cold morning with a gathering of heavily clad protestors on the U.S. Capitol grounds that kept expanding wider and wider as the hours, then the minutes went on. The New Mobilization Committee to End the War in Vietnam, which was also called the New Mobe, had planned well for what it called the Vietnam Moratorium.

The morning chill had ended and at 10:00 a.m. the cue was given to move forward, going northwest up Pennsylvania Avenue, and by that time the gathering of demonstrators had grown to over one-quarter of a million, mainly students but others too, including many representatives of labor unions, forming an attendance of the largest protest ever held in Washington, D.C.

They marched some twenty abreast up the Avenue, many with black armbands, continually shouting familiar chants and some not so familiar. The North Vietnamese and Viet Cong flags were back from a month earlier, as were the upside-down flags of the United States.

Even when the lead of the demonstration reached the Federal Trade Commission on Pennsylvania and 6th, the rear of the procession was not yet in sight. Numbers were chilling in both sight and sound, with the participants now yelling "Smash the State!" and "One, two, three, four! We don't want your [obscenity] war!" But those chants were not made to the exclusion of "Ho! Ho! Ho Chih Minh! The N.L.F. is Going to Win!" Repetition, in itself, was intended to be frightening, and it was.

When two blocks further were reached, they were outside the U.S. Department of Justice and they came to a halt that was unexpected to observers. The reason for the halt became quickly apparent as many protesters started beating at the walls and the doors while other protestors broke its windows. Over 40 people were arrested. Then the flag of the United States above the U.S. Department of Justice was ripped down from its flagpole and it was set on fire. The flag of the Viet Cong was raised.

Some protesters threw rocks and bottles and other things

at the police. The police then used tear-gas, which set most protesters to run across the street to the wide staircase outside the Old Post Office Building. On that wide staircase they held banners with profane words on them in some kind of slogan difficult to figure out, and they screamed so many profanities that the chants became intermingled and became more noise than separated messages. When the tear-gas breeze followed them on the staircase, the group scattered.

A young couple was running down 12th Street by the parking lot between the Old Post Office Building and the Internal Revenue Service. The couple was locked in role-reversal, the young man not just crying but sobbing, while the young woman was comforting him with her arm around him. They slowed their run down to a walk as they were far enough away from the effects of the tear-gas.

"Are you okay?" a stranger asked.

"No! No! I'm not okay!" the young man answered and then poured out a blurted sob. In one of his hands was a rolled up handkerchief, and the other hand was gripped around a rock. On his shirt was a picture of Che Guevara, the deceased Latin American revolutionary. The young man also wore a black-and-white checkered cloth headband, and around his neck was a necklace with a large pendant in the shape of a peace symbol. His girlfriend wore no jewelry at all but did wear a leather jacket adorned with a number of painted peace symbols in different colors that were beginning to crumble since she had obviously painted them on the leather with a felt-tip marker.

"What's up?" the stranger asked.

The young man's sobbing was so intense that he couldn't answer, but the young woman did. "The police!"

"You mean the tear-gas?"

"The death-gas! That's like Hitler did in the concentration camps!"

The stranger couldn't help but smile. "Oh, I don't think so. I've been breathing in the tear-gas, too. It's sharp and it sure isn't comfortable, but I think we'll all live through it."

Then the young man regained some composure and between sobs he was able to say, "Why did they do that? Why did they do that to me?!"

"Honey, you'll be okay," his girlfriend said as she rubbed her hand on his arm, continuing to comfort him.

It was very apparent to the stranger that the girlfriend seemed much better able to handle all this than her boyfriend. "How come the tear-gas didn't bother you?" the stranger asked the young woman.

"Oh, it bothered me a lot, but it's a little better now. We got away from the pigs in time! Henry and Donna really got it because they stayed at the front of the Justice Department when we got away from there. That's where we were at."

"Henry and Donna? I don't know them."

"The four of us were with a whole bunch of friends from Chicago."

"Well, do you think all your friends are lying dead from the tear-gas in the street outside Justice?"

"They might as well be. Did you see the pigs put them in the paddy-wagons?"

The stranger nodded. "Yes. I think they were taking them to Dachau."

"Where?"

"No, no. I'm just talking."

Then her boyfriend was able to ask again, "Why did they do that to me?" And he lifted his hand with the handkerchief and he wiped his eyes, and then blew his nose. "I was just doing the Constitution! That [profanity] Johnson!"

"Nixon!" his girlfriend corrected, since her companion had obviously missed an election. Then she looked back at the stranger. "How did you survive the poison gas? Where were you at?"

The stranger started to answer her but he was interrupted by her boyfriend, who felt it necessary to repeat, "I was just doing the Constitution!"

By this time the demonstration was well dispersed in smaller groups that massed in different parts of the city. One group reached the shopping area of Pennsylvania and 14th and they threw rocks at the windows of Garfinkle's Department Store, the American Express Office, and some twenty or so smaller shops up 14th Street from "F" to "I" Streets, leaving a trail of glass over the sidewalks and streets. A major group was attempting to get to the White House but was met with parked busses that formed a barricade around the perimeter of the White House grounds with no space at all between the busses, their lineage forming a wall.

Then came the entertainment outside the Washington Monument on the Mall, and most of the groups collected there. There were speeches by Dr. Benjamin Spock, Dick Gregory, Senators George McGovern, Eugene McCarthy, and Charles Goodell, and music provided by Peter, Paul, and Mary, members of the cast of *Hair*, Pete Seeger, Arlo Guthrie, and others.

Those celebrities were not children. They had long since passed the age of adolescence, and were in positions of prominence or authority and were chiefly responsible for miseducating many too young to be aware of the consequences they were bringing to others distances away. They *used* the most vulnerable kids; they gave them a quick route to importance with the reward of making news early in life, then catered to the kind of private fun they knew was craved by that age group. Taking advantage of the inexperience that routinely comes with so few years of life is nothing less than political child abuse to enhance a determination of their own.

At dusk there was something new: a procession composed largely of students walking slowly through the streets as they held lighted candles, many of the students with solemn expressions and with tears, displaying what appeared to be grief rather than their yelling of daytime chants. Some created teams of four, each team holding empty coffins to symbolize the dead. Television cameras followed them on their procession and interviewed protestors who spoke of their sadness over "U.S. imperialism."

After sunset their sadness seemed to end when some assembled at Dupont Circle to riot outside the Embassy of the Republic of (South) Vietnam while the great majority reached their destination of West Potomac Park, south of the Lincoln Memorial. The television reporters and camerapersons courteously went away. West Potomac Park was turned into a massive bed of sleeping bags filled with two or more people in them. The boys and girls had what could best be described as a party far from home, and little if any of their dialogue was about

Vietnam. This evening departure was to become a routine that would be repeated from one D.C. demonstration to the next.

Directly across the river from West Potomac Park was Arlington National Cemetery, a graveyard of heroes; but they could hardly see it against the night sky except for the flickering of the Eternal Flame above the grave of President Kennedy, and they likely didn't notice it. That isn't why they came to West Potomac Park. After a long day of demonstration, "Make Love, Not War" was their mantra that validated the dessert of finding strangers for a night of pleasure among the monuments.

For the observer, the acrid odor of marijuana mixed with the pungency of other things became untenable. For the participants in West Potomac Park it was an autumn version of a spring break—better yet, a Spring Break with a Cause. What could be better than that?

They could give a seemingly principled excuse for being out of state and out of sight from those who loved them. There was even guitar music.

8

THE FRAGILE BRIDGE
TO PARIS

IT WAS BAD enough for the U.S. government to have severe difficulties with the government of North Vietnam, and demonstrators in the streets of D.C., but added to those difficulties were self-appointed U.S. representatives traveling to Hanoi, North Vietnam, clearly in violation of the Logan Act that prohibits private, unelected citizens from consulting with foreign governments and attempting to influence them in matters that relate "to any disputes or controversies with the United States, or defeat the measures of the United States."

Prior to her trip to Hanoi, the movie actress Jane Fonda told a University of Michigan audience of some 2,000 students [November 21, 1970], "If you understood what communism was, you would hope, you would pray on your knees that we would some day become communist." At Duke University in North Carolina she repeated what she had said in Michigan, adding, "I, a socialist, think that we should arrive toward a socialist society, all the way to communism."

In July of 1972, one half-year before the Paris Peace Accords were signed, Jane Fonda visited Hanoi, North Vietnam, speaking at her own request on Radio Hanoi. Some excerpts from her broadcasts on Radio Hanoi follow:

"I'm very honored to be a guest in your country, and I loudly condemn the crimes that have been committed by the U.S. government in the name of the American people against your country. A growing number of people in the United States not only demand an end to the war, an end to the bombing, a withdrawal of all U.S. troops, and an end to the support of the Thieu clique, but we identify with the struggle of your people. We have understood that we have a common enemy: U.S. imperialism . . .

"I want to publicly accuse Nixon of being a new-type Hitler whose crimes are being unveiled. I want to publicly charge that while waging the war of aggression in Vietnam he has betrayed everything the American people have at heart. The tragedy is for the United States and not for the Vietnamese people, because the Vietnamese people will soon regain their independence and freedom . . .

"To the U.S. servicemen who are stationed on the aircraft carriers in the Gulf of Tonkin, those of you who load the bombs on the planes should know that those weapons are illegal. And the use of those bombs or condoning the use of those bombs makes one a war criminal.

"I'm not a pacifist. I understand why the Vietnamese are fighting . . . against a white man's racist aggression. We know what U.S. imperialism has done to our country so we know what lies in store for any third-world country that could have the misfortune of falling into the hands of a country such as the United States and becoming a colony . . . You know that when Nixon says the war is winding down, that he's lying . . . I think Richard Nixon would do well to read Vietnamese history, particularly their poetry, and particularly the poetry written by Ho Chi Minh."

Jane Fonda wasn't the only one to visit Hanoi in protest of U.S. policy: Tom Hayden, Ramsey Clark, and others visited Hanoi during the war and met with U.S. prisoners of war selected by their captors. Those prisoners who were selected but refused to see the visitors were severely tortured.

On Jane Fonda's return to the United States she said that "They are the best treated prisoners in history."

Ramsey Clark, like Jane Fonda, made a propaganda broadcast over Radio Hanoi while he was in Hanoi, in his case traveling there for a Swedish group called "Revealing U.S. Crimes in Indochina." On his return to the United States, Clark said the American prisoners "were unquestionably humanely treated, well treated," and their living conditions "could not be better." The health of the American prisoners are "better than mine, and I am a healthy man."

[Between 1965 and 1973 the Red Cross carried out 475 inspections of Prisoner of War camps in South Vietnam, while North Vietnam refused even one inspection of their Prisoner of War camps.]

The travelers to Hanoi compounded the fragility of the bridge to Paris, but the most surprising vulnerability to the signing of the Paris Peace Accords beyond the travelers, beyond the demonstrators, beyond the intransigence of the North Vietnam

Government, was the unpredicted difficulties with President Thieu of *South* Vietnam.

President Thieu was justifiably concerned (proven right) that the North Vietnamese and the Viet Cong would increase their receipt of arms from their allies beyond the one-to-one requirement. Additionally, he was just as concerned (with validity) at our lack of demanding that all North Vietnamese troops in South Vietnam return home. [They were often mixed with Viet Cong posing independence from North Vietnam, as referred to earlier in Chapter Six.] There were other charges, frequently made by associates of President Thieu [and of no validity]. President Nixon then made some adjustments to the draft of the proposed agreement, but neither of the two leaders predicted that their biggest obstacle would be the United States Congress, which would simply ignore the provisions of the Accords and ignore the signature on letters of President Nixon when he wrote to President Thieu.

Without either of them knowing that biggest obstacle to come, the correspondence between President Nixon and President Thieu became increasingly angry prior to the signing of the Accords during the last quarter of 1972 into January of 1973.

EXCERPTS OF PRESIDENT NIXON'S LETTERS TO PRESIDENT THIEU REGARDING U.S. DISAPPOINTMENT IN POSITIONS OF PRESIDENT THIEU:

[October 6, 1972]
"I would urge you to take every measure to avoid the development of an atmosphere which could lead to events similar to

those which we abhorred in 1963 and which I personally op-
posed so vehemently in 1968." [He is referring to events in South
Vietnam that culminated in the assassination of President Ngo
Dinh Diem.]

[November 8, 1972]

"I must first of all express my deep disappointment over what
I consider to be a dangerous drift in the relationship between our
two countries, a tendency which can only undercut our mutual ob-
jectives and benefit the enemy. Your continuing distortions of the
agreement and attacks upon it are unfair and self-defeating. These
have persisted despite our numerous representations . . . They have
been disconcerting and highly embarrassing to me . . . The charges
made by some of your associates are becoming more and more
incomprehensible."

[November 14, 1972]

"If, on the other hand, we are unable to agree on the course
that I have outlined, it is difficult for me to see how we will be
able to continue our common effort towards securing a just and
honorable peace. As General Haig told you I would with great
reluctance be forced to consider other alternatives. For this rea-
son, it is essential that we have your agreement as we proceed
into our next meeting with Hanoi's negotiators. And I strongly
urge you and your advisors to work promptly with Ambassa-
dor Bunker and our Mission in Saigon on the many practical
problems which will face us in implementing the agreement. I
cannot overemphasize the urgency of the task at hand nor my
unalterable determination to proceed along the course which we
have outlined."

[November 23, 1972]

*"Given my clear messages and those conveyed by my represen-
tatives these past several weeks, any further delay from your side
can only be interpreted as an effort to scuttle the agreement. This
would have a disastrous effect on our ability to continue to support
you and your Government. I look forward to seeing your emissary
in Washington as soon as the Paris sessions have been concluded,
but in the interim I must urge you this last time not to put ourselves irrevocably at odds. If the current course continues and you
fail to join us in concluding a satisfactory agreement with Hanoi,
you must understand that I will proceed at whatever the cost."*

[December 17, 1972]

*"I am convinced that your refusal to join us would be an in-
vitation to disaster to the loss of all that we together have fought
over the past decade. It would be inexcusable above all because we
will have lost a just and honorable alternative."*

[January 5, 1973]

*"We have explained to you repeatedly why we believe the prob-
lem of North Vietnamese troops is manageable under the agreement, and I see no reason to repeat all the arguments."*

[January 15, 1973]

*(If you do not agree) "I shall have to explain publicly that
your government obstructs peace. The result will be an inevitable
and immediate termination of U.S. economic and military assistance which cannot be forestalled by a change of personnel in
your government. I hope, however, that after all our two countries
have shared and suffered together in conflict, we will stay together*

to preserve peace and reap its benefits. To this end I want to repeat to you the assurances that I have already conveyed. At the time of the signing of the agreement I will make emphatically clear that the United States recognizes your government as the only legal government of South Vietnam, that we do not recognize the right of any foreign troops to be present on South Vietnam territory, and that we will react strongly in the event the agreement is violated. Finally, I want to emphasize my continued commitment to the freedom and progress of the Republic of Vietnam. It is my firm intention to continue full economic and military aid."

[January 20, 1973]

"It is obvious that we face a situation on a new basis. It is obvious that we face a situation of most extreme gravity when long-time friends of South Vietnam such as Senators Goldwater and Stennis, on whom we have relied for four years to carry our programs of assistance through the Congress, make public declarations that a refusal by your Government of reasonable peace terms would make it impossible to continue aid. It is this situation which now threatens everything for which our two countries have suffered so much . . . As I have told you, we will initial the Agreement on January 23. I must know now whether you are prepared to join us in this course, and I must have your answer by 12:00 Washington time, January 21, 1973. I must meet with key Congressional leaders Sunday evening, January 21 to inform them in general terms of our course. If you cannot give me a positive answer by then, I shall inform them that I am authorizing Dr. Kissinger to initial the Agreement even without the concurrence of your Government . . . Finally and most importantly, I must have your assurances now, on the most

personal basis, that when we initial the Agreement on Tuesday we will be doing so in the knowledge that you will proceed to sign the Agreement jointly with us. The Agreement, I assure you, will represent the beginning of a new period of close collaboration and strong mutual support between the Republic of Vietnam and the United States. You and I will work together in peacetime to protect the independence and freedom of your country as we have done in war. If we close ranks now and proceed together, we will prevail."

EXCERPTS OF PRESIDENT NIXON'S LETTERS TO PRESIDENT THIEU REGARDING U.S. ASSURANCE OF CONTINUED AID AND ASSURANCE OF U.S. REPONSE TO ANY NORTH VIETNAMESE AGGRESSION:

[October 16, 1972]

"In the period following the cessation of hostilities you can be completely assured that we will continue to provide your Government with the fullest support, including continued economic aid and whatever military assistance is consistent with the ceasefire provisions of this Government . . . I can assure you that we will view any breach of faith on their part with the utmost gravity, and it would have the most serious consequences."

[Excerpt Added in President Nixon's handwriting] "I am personally convinced it is the best we will be able to get and that the GVN [South Vietnam] must survive as a free country."

[November 8, 1972]

"I have repeatedly given firm guarantees against the possibility that the agreement is violated."

[November 14, 1972]

"You have my absolute assurance that if Hanoi fails to abide by the terms of this agreement it is my intention to take swift and severe retaliatory action ... I repeat my personal assurance to you that the United States will react very strongly and rapidly to any violation of the agreement."

[January 5, 1973]

"Should you decide, as I trust you will, to go with us, you have my assurance of continued assistance in the post-settlement period and that we will respond with full force should the settlement be violated by North Vietnam. So once more I conclude with an appeal to you to close ranks with us."

In President Nixon's letter to President Thieu of January 20, 1973 (the same day as President Nixon's Second Inaugural), he accented seven particular clauses in the agreement that should give assurance to President Thieu:

The affirmation of the independence and sovereignty of South Vietnam [Articles 14, 18e, and 20.]

The provision for reunification only by peaceful means, through agreement and without coercion or annexation, which establishes the illegitimacy of any use or threat of force in the name of reunification [Article 15].

The U.S. and DRV, on an equal basis, pledging themselves against any outside interference in the exercise of the South Vietnamese people's right to self-determination [Article 9].

The legal prohibition of the introduction of troops, advisers, and war material into South Vietnam from outside South Vietnam [Article 7].

The principle of respect for the demilitarized zone and the provisional military demarcation line [Article 15].

The prohibition of the use of Laotian and Cambodian territory to encroach upon the sovereignty and security of South Vietnam [Article 20].

The fact that all Communist forces [this phrase intentionally makes no separation between the Viet Cong and North Vietnamese] in South Vietnam are subject to the obligation that their reduction and demobilization are to be negotiated as soon as possible [Article 13].

Then he once again requested that President Thieu close ranks.

President Thieu closed ranks. The Accords would be signed by the Government of South Vietnam.

At President Nixon's invitation, on April the 2nd of 1973, a little over two months after the signing of the Paris Peace Accords, President and Mrs. Thieu of South Vietnam were welcomed at Casa Pacifica in San Clemente, California, which was known as the Western White House.

It was 10:30 in the morning when President Thieu was received. Excerpts follow from the welcome of President Nixon: "Mr. President, this is the fifth time that I have had the honor and pleasure of meeting with you, but for the first time I am honored to welcome you in my native land in my native State, and here at my home. As we welcome you today, we think back to the times we have met before. Particularly I think of the time that we first met as heads of state at Midway, four years ago. On that occasion, you said after our meeting that you looked forward to the time when we could meet not for the purpose of discussing the conduct of war, but for the purpose of discussing the building of peace. And now, today, that day has come. There are, of course, difficulties in building a peace after 25 years of war have torn your country apart. But on the other hand, when we compare the situation today to what it was four years ago at Midway when we met, we see the progress that has been made toward that goal. On that day, when there were over half a million Americans fighting side by side with your people, we now find that all the American forces have returned, and the people of Vietnam have the strength to defend their own independence and their right to choose their government in the years ahead . . .

"I would say simply, as we conclude, that the name of our house here is Casa Pacifica, which means House of the Pacific, and also House of Peace, and we hope from this day, as a result of our talks, will come great steps forward in building the lasting peace, the real peace that we have fought together for and that now we want all of our people to live for.

"Thank you."

Excerpts follow from the response of President Thieu: "Mr. President, Mrs. Nixon, ladies and gentlemen: Thank you very much, Mr. President, for this warm welcome and for your very kind words. Mrs. Thieu and I are very happy to come here today to this beautiful land of freedom and prosperity. We appreciate most especially your hospitality. I find it very significant that the discussions which I will soon hold with you on this visit, which will establish the new basis for the cooperation between the United States and Vietnam, following the Vietnam peace agreement, are to be held in the Western White House on the Pacific Coast, because both the United States and Vietnam belong to the same community of nations bordering on the Pacific Ocean ...

"Mr. President, over three years ago, when we met at Midway, at a time when the Vietnam war was raging, we laid down together the foundations for a promising solution to the Vietnam conflict that came to be known as the Vietnamization. Today, while over 300,000 American troops still stay in Europe to bolster the defense of Western Europe more than a quarter century after World War II was over, we in Vietnam are proud that, thanks to your help, the Vietnamese defense force was able to repel an all-out Communist invasion last year, at a time when American ground troops had been withdrawn.

"This made possible a peace with honor whereby the Communist aggressors, in the Paris agreement last January, had to recognize formally the right of self-determination of the people of South Vietnam and the principle that the problems we will solve in North Vietnam are to be solved by peaceful means, without coercion and annexation. While the road to lasting peace is still an arduous one, a new page has been turned with the conclusion of the Paris agreement, and I look forward to having fruitful conversation with you, Mr. President, on the various aspects of the relation between our two countries in this new context.

"I earnestly hope that the joint efforts of our two governments would lead to a consolidation of peace in Indochina and a new era of constructive cooperation in peace among all parties concerned. I avail myself on this occasion to express to you, Mr. President, and through you to the American people, the heartfelt gratitude of the Vietnamese Government and people for the generous assistance of your government and the noble contribution of the American nation to our long efforts to defend and preserve freedom for Vietnam and Southeast Asia.

"Thank you very much."

Future policy-makers might find value in studying the communications written to a foreign president [recorded in this chapter on earlier pages] by a President of the United States, knowing now what happened when a new U.S. President and a new U.S. Congress came into office. In the United States, as well as other democracies, the word of its leader given to a foreign power has traditionally and wisely been kept by the nation's future leadership. The promises of a president of a democracy to a foreign nation has always been assumed to have been the word not of one person, but of one nation.

President Thieu was proven right by his concern of leaving North Vietnamese troops anywhere within the borders of South Vietnam, while President Nixon was right in promising aid from the United States should there be North Vietnamese aggression. And both Presidents were wrong in not foreseeing the possibility that a future congress of the United States would break the promises made, and that a future president would be unable or unwilling to accept the domestic consequences of keeping the promises. In this case, promises made to a foreign power were broken and surrender followed. To prevent such possibilities in the future, anything short of unconditional surrender or total destruction of the enemy gives opportunity to the enemy to attack again, and gives it the ability to achieve its ultimate victory. It happened. The purpose of entering a war must always be to win. Nothing less.

Not ever.

* * *

Move the calendar to Christmas Day of 1978. That was when the victors of Vietnam [by this time called the Socialist Republic of Vietnam] launched an invasion of 200,000 troops into Cambodia. Thirteen days later, on January 7, 1979, the Vietnamese troops succeeded in ousting the government of the Khmer Rouge. It was extremely welcome news since no one else had done it or would do it. But Vietnam replaced the Khmer Rouge with a Vietnam-dictated government run by Heng Samrin. Hell had a new master. There was no friendship or trust between Cambodia and Vietnam, but Cambodians, knowing full well they had a new master, had more than justified relief that the Khmer Rouge was replaced as the ruling government.

In October of 1980 there was a contest in the United Nations to decide what government should be recognized by the U.N. as the legal government of Cambodia. The choice offered was to retain the U.N. membership of the Khmer Rouge supported by the People's Republic of China or, instead, give recognition to the Heng Samrin Government put in place by the Socialist Republic of Vietnam and supported by the Soviet Union.

After the vote was taken, the winner shook hands to thank the U.S. delegate to the U.N. for the vote of the U.S. The U.S. delegate, Robert Rosenstock, said that he felt like washing his hands after that. He should have. Under direction from the U.S. State Department, he voted for the Khmer Rouge.

Even under the choices given to the members of the U.N. General Assembly, there were other courses that could have been taken by the United States: we could have joined 32 other nations that abstained from voting for either of the two governments or, best of all, we could have kept our hands entirely clean by stepping beyond the choices offered. We could have taken advantage of the circumstances by voting for a Cambodian Government in Exile composed of the leadership of those who wanted a free Cambodia and had escaped from Cambodia into refuge after the Khmer Rouge takeover in 1975.

It would have been important that as long as the United States retained membership in the U.N., the actions and votes of the United States within that international organization would have been those of principle, no matter the resistance and condemnations by others.

Now move the calendar to July 11, 1995, some twenty years after the fall of South Vietnam, when President Clinton announced the establishment of full diplomatic relations between the United States and the Government of the Socialist Republic of Vietnam. Giving such recognition signaled to others that it is unnecessary for a foreign government to keep its agreements with the United States.

Although it was too late to correct the errors of the 94th Congress, it was not too late to insist that the Vietnamese Government observe the freedoms they guaranteed to the South Vietnamese in the Paris Peace Accords. We could have told Vietnam's Prime Minister Vo Van Kiet that we would recognize his government the day it keeps its word. Our diplomatic recognition without first insisting that the Socialist Republic of Vietnam observe its own signature was another wound to those Americans who served, and to their families, and to those whose loved ones will never come back.

9

KINGS AND QUEENS OF D.C.'S INVISIBLE MONARCHY

THE D.C. BUREAUCRACIES are not champions of creativity. Their suggestion for the name of the U.S. homecoming of the Prisoners of War was "Operation Egress Recap." Egress Recap? What the devil does that mean? Happily, the White House intervened and changed the name to Operation Homecoming.

But that isn't the most serious fault with the bureaucracy:

It is generally assumed that during the Southeast Asian War, the bureaucracy of the United States Government worked in concert with the President of the United States to support U.S. policy. That assumption is inaccurate.

Within each of the great stone buildings in the District of Columbia that house the mammoth bureaucracies, there is a secret. The secret is that D.C. has a permanent government led by an Invisible Monarchy. The Invisible Monarchy is composed of the highest ranking Civil Service and Foreign Service careerists who stay in government while presidents of the nation come and go. Since any new president of the United States inherits rather than appoints over 95 percent of those who work in the departments, agencies, and bureaus of the Executive Branch, those inherited Civil Service and Foreign Service officers see themselves as the permanent government. That bureaucracy of some two million regards those highest ranking careerists as the Kings and Queens and Princes and Princesses within each department and agency and bureau.

They didn't get to be Kings and Queens and Princes and Princesses for nothing. Achieving those crowns took fighting for assignment to assignment and post to post, maintaining, through the years, a political outlook held in common with those higher up in the royalty. That's because in the years in which they struggle to get higher in the rank, those above them who are already crowned give the lower echelons their performance reports, and determine their status in grade and pay. The President and the appointees of their departments don't know those in the lower echelons. The Kings and Queens and Princes and Princesses know who they are. And so those who are new to the bureaucracy most often implement the President's decisions only if the President's decisions match the policies of their direct superiors in the Invisible Monarchy. And when they eventually receive the crowns themselves, having become a real King or Queen or Prince or Princess with followers beneath them, they will not willingly abdicate their positions because of a mere election. And so the political outlook of the throne is permanent no matter the will of the voters.

And the system goes on and on. Unsurprisingly, that's the

way it was through much of the Foreign Service during the most controversial years of the Southeast Asian War. The elected Presidents had little allegiance from their own foreign policy bureaucracies.

There was the Foreign Service Officer who was posted in Karachi, Pakistan, who said, "I never mention Vietnam here unless someone asks me. And then I just tell them the truth: it's a civil war and we have no business being there."

There was the Foreign Service Officer who was posted in Rome who said to a resident of the host nation, "'I served in Rome before. Back in 1961 I saw big red banners saying 'Vota Communista.' I was surprised, but then I learned why they had those banners. This country still has the biggest Communist Party in Western Europe. And it isn't all a protest vote like everyone in Washington wants you to think. Communism might well be the only thing that could stabilize this country and end the fragmentation of strikes and political and social chaos. If they ask my opinion about politics I just say I have no comment. They know what that means. And when they ask what's going on in America, I tell them the best man can't always win in our system."

There was the Foreign Service Officer who was posted at the U.S. Embassy in Dar es Salaam who said, "Do you know what I tell the Tanzanians? I tell them we call him Tricky Dick. They laugh. There was a demonstration against Nixon around the Embassy last month. Some of our Peace Corps young people were in that demonstration. I told them I was with them and I wore black that day to identify to the Tanzanians that I was with the demonstrators."

There was the Foreign Service Officer who served in the

U.S. Embassy in Caracas who said to a resident of Venezuela, "I think of Nixon what you think of President Caldera. Neither one of us knows what a true democracy is. But we can see what our governments do to our countries. I'm not spreading any of that anti-Castro propaganda I get from Washington. Castro might be better for his country than Caldera is for your country or Nixon is for mine."

There was the Foreign Service Officer who was posted in Nairobi, Kenya, who said, "When a visitor comes from Washington I put the picture of Nixon right-side up. When he leaves, I hang it back upside-down. Those students from Kenyatta College laugh when they see it upside-down. I relate to them. They're the coming leaders of the African continent. They aren't as with-the-times as our students back home, but they're learning."

There was the Foreign Service Officer in Ibadan, Nigeria, who said, "When Nixon gave that Silent Majority speech I thought I'd barf. I didn't tell the locals here that Humphrey supported Nixon on that. I wanted to give the people some hope about America."

All of this deserves context: there are Foreign Service Officers who are marvelous and who follow the policies of the President whether or not they share those convictions.

Moreover, being a U.S. Foreign Service Officer can be a dangerous career that can become commensurate with those in uniform. The diplomats who were held for 444 days in Iran as hostages of the Iranian Fundamentalist Revolutionary Government are well known, but the same year in which our Embassy in Iran and its diplomats were captured, U.S. Ambassador to Afghanistan Adolph "Spike" Dubs was abducted by extremists in

Kabul, then brought to a hotel where he was murdered [February 14, 1979]. His assassination was hardly the first or the last for the Foreign Service.

Although Foreign Service Officers can request to be posted in a particular foreign site, they often find themselves in places that are geographically and politically far from their requested destination.

Before given a foreign assignment, Foreign Service Officers are given a 38-page booklet, printed and distributed by the U.S. Department of State, entitled, *Hostage Taking: Preparation, Avoidance, and Survival.* The title explains well its purpose. Its list of instructions before going overseas include: "Update your will ... Make sure all insurance policies are up to date ... Consider establishing trust funds for dependents ... " But those are elementary compared to the rest of it.

Section Three contains some warnings about terrorists and potential capture by them: "They have not had the opportunity to get to know you as an individual, so they will feel no compunction about killing you if it serves their purposes to do so ... This option may suit their purposes nearly as well as the hostage taking would have ... Often they will try to isolate you from events by placing you in a darkened cell or otherwise denying you all sensory output, removing your sense of time ... Occasionally hostages are kept in an unsanitary environment, dehumanized by being called by a number, or other designation other than their name, provided inadequate or no hygiene or bathroom facilities, deprived of sleep, and given poor or insufficient food."

Most of the booklet gives advice on how best the captured should handle themselves so as to increase their chances of survival.

None of this, including their heroism, should be dismissed, nor should there be dismissal of those Foreign Service Officers who, when faced with a difference between the policy convictions of the President and their own convictions, lean toward what they would like to see as policy, done by some with subtlety and by others with blatancy.

What so many Foreign Service Officers did during the Southeast Asian War was a logical extension that started much earlier in the foreign service in a different part of the world. It was 1948 and it was the Truman Administration. The place was Israel. In that U.S. Administration and in forthcoming administrations, Presidents of the United States supported the State of Israel in its conflicts with its neighboring Arab States. The State Department made necessary *public* statements of support for that policy, but generally the State Department bureaucracy did not support that view. It was not because the U.S. State Department held a politically strategic or religion-based or race-based bias against Israel. Their reasoning was human-nature-based and, unfortunately, was not overcome: they wanted to have a career that was fun, or at least not terrible. They had already chosen a livelihood that would bring them to foreign posts throughout their working years; often a succession of two-year posts, with some of them lasting longer. With 21 Arab countries and 20 other Moslem countries and only one Israel, the odds were high that the U.S. Foreign Service Officer would serve in any number of Arab or other Islamic countries during a career, and probably not serve in Israel at all. Life is easier for a U.S. diplomat when posted to a country whose government endorses U.S. policies, rather than in a country whose citizens are throwing bricks at the U.S. Embassy—and at times throwing bricks at those who work for the Embassy. Don't bother looking for a more principled justification in that position of those Foreign Service Officers. There isn't any.

Not always, but generally in time, even Secretaries of State, like other Cabinet Officers, find themselves departing from their original intent of supporting the President's policies and, instead, becoming followers of the beliefs and policies of the careerists. Life is easier that way. They find themselves spending time with their bureaucracy on a daily basis. They see the President by appointment. Their bureaucracy appears to be composed of experts. After all, there are always those Foreign Service Officers who lived in Kuala Lumpur or Prague or Ouagadougou—or Saigon. It is unlikely that the President spent years in those places.

Moreover, there is the likelihood that Cabinet Officers, in addition to becoming willing victims of bureaucrats and victims of their own weaknesses, will become victims of the geography of the District of Columbia. They work in the departments they are supposed to supervise, and so they are located in their separate buildings, usually bigger than the White House, and they have separate staffs, usually bigger than the staff of the White House. Their physical surroundings, as well as their advisors, give them distance from the President.

The White House staff, on the other hand, is where the President is located. They have the day-to-day knowledge of where the President wants to go, and their job is to see that he gets there. That is what the Cabinet Officers are supposed to do too, but they are busy being the chiefs in their own worlds, with the President down the street or more likely a mile or so away, not knowing what's going on inside those buildings.

Even appointed Ambassadors are susceptible to the disease: the Ambassador often becomes more of an advocate of the host country to which he or she is appointed rather than an advocate of the U.S. President's policies. It happens because an Ambassador can easily start having devotion and an allegiance to the country of appointment and therefore try to convince the President of the importance of that country. Moreover, if that country is not all that important, then neither is the Ambassador all that important. In the days of the Southeast Asian War, most Ambassadors found themselves in foreign nations that opposed U.S. involvement in that war. Unlike the United States, most nations did not have the tradition of fighting for the liberty of strangers, and their governments did not understand such policies.

Many U.S. Ambassadors found their team of Foreign Service Officers were hesitant to speak ill of the Soviet Union or of Communism, because the host nation veered to the side of Communism or were categorized as "third-world nations" that did not take an official side in the struggle between liberty and Communism. And many Foreign Service Officers simply wanted to "get along" with the locals, and justified their "getting along" as doing their job.

There was even a recommendation from Foreign Service Officers of the State Department that instead of posting a flag of the United States on the moon, we should implant a flag of the United Nations. And if there should be a plaque left on the moon it should have the signature of the U.N.'s Secretary General engraved on it, not the President of the United States. The recommendations were rejected.

In contrast to discussing our involvement in Vietnam, Foreign Service Officers stressed our space explorations in the countries to which they were posted because U.S. space exploration was so greatly admired and faced little controversy. Apollo was easy to "sell." Vietnam wasn't easy to "sell," and so they chose not to do it. By the silence of our own officers, there was no overseas reservoir of understanding about Vietnam. Our officers often explained that their silence regarding Vietnam was due to the countries in which they were posted having no interest in Vietnam. One of our overseas officers was asked if he would talk about our Apollo missions if the locals there weren't interested in them.

He said, "Yes, of course."

When asked why he would do that, he admitted that he talked about Apollo because he was so proud of it, and space exploration was a great American mission.

"And Vietnam?" he was asked.

He answered, "Please tell the President that Vietnam makes my job more difficult."

When the officer was told that the *officer's* decisions made the *President's* job more difficult, it was greeted with a closed-lips smile and a condescending nod.

In 1971 the United States Information Agency (U.S.I.A.) completed production on a feature-length motion picture on Vietnam whose planning had started back in 1968 during President Johnson's Administration. As was true of all U.S.I.A. films, it was made exclusively for foreign release. It was, perhaps, the only documentary film from any U.S. source that advocated the U.S. position in defense of South Vietnam. The motion picture was entitled, *Vietnam! Vietnam!* John Ford, the giant of Hollywood filmmaking, volunteered to be the executive producer, John Hynd was the producer, Sherman Beck was the director, Tom Duggan wrote the screenplay, and Charlton Heston was the narrator. Most of its cinematography took place in South Vietnam with some segments shot in the United States.

Much of the U.S. Foreign Service did not want the film made and voiced opposition to it. If completed, its exhibition by the Foreign Service in foreign lands was questionable, but both the Johnson and Nixon Administrations went ahead with it.

Many of the spontaneous quotes from the soundtrack of the film are worth reviving to give a flavor of the film and its fate. All the following excerpts from the film were said by people appearing before the cameras.

THE WIFE OF A PRISONER OF WAR: "We are very puzzled about why they [the North Vietnamese Government] won't tell us whether or not the men are alive or dead. It seems a very simple thing for them to do. They have told many wives to come back and demonstrate against the government—against the U.S. government—and they implied that we should join the 'Women's Strike for Peace' and that this would be the most helpful thing that we could do to help our men.

"Once we educate the general public not only in this nation but worldwide to the true facts, these men are in fact not being treated the way Hanoi would like to paint the picture, then I believe public pressure will be brought to bear upon Hanoi and they will be shown up for the dishonesty and untruths that they are putting forth.

"And tell the world we have not heard—we do not know. Please just let us know if our husbands or sons are alive. This is so little to ask."

A SECOND WIFE OF A PRISONER OF WAR: "I've gone to see Senator McGovern since he has been to Paris and talked with the North Vietnamese; I have written to Secretary General U Thant at the U.N. and I have written Xuan Thuy [North Vietnam's chief negotiator in Paris] several times and have never received a reply."

A THIRD WIFE OF A PRISONER OF WAR: "In one of my most recent letters to Senator Fulbright I said, 'Last summer I wrote to you asking for an appointment with you and expressing the idea that the most vociferous critics of the war had probably lengthened the war and thus had a detrimental effect on the possibility of release for prisoners. At that time, you refused to see me on the grounds that my idea was so preposterous,' and that was his phrase, 'that visiting with me would serve no purpose.'

"We are going back today to Paris in hopes of finding the information we originally went there seeking. On September 17, the North Vietnamese promised to send to us letters regarding our husbands' status and well-being. We have not to date received those letters. We still want to know about our husbands; what we can tell our children concerning their fathers."

The following excerpts are from a montage of varied opinions regarding U.S. policy:

YOUNG WOMAN STUDENT: "I lost a very good friend over there and all of a sudden it brought it home to me and I began wondering, what are we doing over there? Is this what honor is all about? Is it worth it? And I don't think it is."

DR. BENJAMIN SPOCK: "We believe that this war is illegal from every point of view, completely immoral; and I would like to add for myself that it is detrimental to the best interests of the United States."

REPORTER TO WOUNDED G.I. IN HOSPITAL: "Do you feel that what you've gone through and that you have to go through the rest of your life was worthwhile?"
WOUNDED G.I.: "Yes, I do. Because I think just all people should think of just one thing right now and that's freedom. And the only way we are going to get freedom is to protect ourselves, whether it's in this country or in other countries that need our help. And I think a lot of people feel the same way as I do."

SENATOR EUGENE MCCARTHY, in reference to prospective killings by the Communists in Southeast Asia, should they win the war: "I don't think there is any evidence or any real evidence or any reason to believe that that kind of mass execution would take place."

GOVERNOR RONALD REAGAN: "The very fact that practically two million of the North Vietnamese fled to South

Vietnam to escape the Communist regime is an indication that this government did not represent the will of the people."

SENATOR CHARLES GOODELL: "Not only are we bleeding our men, letting them die in Vietnam, we are spending a rate of 30 billion dollars a year; two and a half billion dollars a month in Vietnam. And that's more than we spend on our housing program, that's more than we spend on our poverty program in a year. And this money must be diverted back to our domestic needs and we must end this futile war—immoral war."

FORMER SECRETARY OF STATE DEAN RUSK: "What I could do with is more compassion and more sympathy for those tens of thousands of civilians in South Vietnam who have been killed and kidnapped by the Viet Cong and North Vietnamese forces as a matter of deliberate policy, and the far larger tens of thousands of South Vietnamese military who have been killed and wounded simply because North Vietnam is trying to seize South Vietnam by force."

REPORTER: "Have the authorities taken any action against you because of your burning your [draft] card in Central Park in New York?"

YOUNG MAN: "None whatsoever."

REPORTER: "How do you feel about those who say that you're delaying the war, and continuing the war and prolonging it, with this kind of action?"

YOUNG MAN: "We want the war to stop and we feel the best way for the war to stop is for the United States to get out of Vietnam."

GOVERNOR NELSON ROCKEFELLER: "Can you imagine a protestor in Hanoi—how far he would get if he wanted to protest North Vietnam sending troops into South Vietnam, or into Laos or Cambodia? He'd end up in the jug, at best."

HUNGARIAN MAN on Saigon Street to visiting U.S. demonstrators: "You stupid idiots! Never mind my name. I'm a Hungarian Freedom Fighter. You bastards. Those idiots. You stupid idiots. I would shoot you all like the Russians will shoot you if they come. And half of you have no jobs. You hang around the streets all day, you demonstrators. You should be out working or do something in the hospitals. It's a disgrace what you are doing here against your own country. I am ashamed for America and I am not American. I'm a Hungarian."

GIRL IN CROWD: "The people who have died in this war –"

THE HUNGARIAN: "There are many people who died. People died since time immemorial. It is nothing new in people dying for their freedom. People have to die for their children, for their future so they're free. Americans like you here now—you couldn't walk around in Peking. Because you are misled. Deep inside I'm sure you're all very, very decent people. You want the best for humanity, but humanity is finished in the communist countries. You people should not be shot; that is too good for you. Do you know what it means having communists? Go to Hungary. Go to Czechoslovakia. Go to East—Don't laugh so idiotically in the back. Don't run away now. You should listen to that. Stupid idiots. The people here are fighting for your freedom. Every coolie here is a hero. Every coolie, every Vietnamese should get a medal. Every American who works or fights here is a hero. You will realize when it is too late."

Very few people saw the film, as many U.S. Foreign Service Officers stationed overseas (whose duty was to promote U.S. foreign policy) found it easier to ignore Vietnam. The claim was made that "we tried." As a result, *Vietnam! Vietnam!* was shortly withdrawn and put in the archives.

A brave man, Abraham Brumberg, became the founder and editor of a bi-monthly magazine titled *Problems of Communism* for the United States Information Agency whose superiors in the bureaucracy of the U.S.I.A. fought against the publication. During earlier years, the Agency had a standing rule to prevent the use of criticisms against leading Communists: Stalin, Lenin, Marx, or Engels. But Abraham Brumberg bucked the Invisible Monarchy. When the Cold War was over, Brumberg admitted, "My colleagues and I simply disregarded the instructions. Eventually common sense prevailed. But this was a mark of the times; lunatic but not all that unusual."

During the heart of the Southeast Asian War, the same superiors of the bureaucracy fought against the release of a U.S.I.A. film (made without their knowledge) on the 1968 Soviet invasion of Czechoslovakia. Due to the uniquely strong new director of the Agency, Frank Shakespeare, the bureaucracy was forced to release the film, as he overrode their veto. To the disappointment of many of the top-ranking Foreign Service Officers and Civil Service Officers of the Agency and the State Department (and to Communist Governments), the clearly anti-Soviet film was exhibited widely by foreign distributors, and received massive audiences.

A particularly glowing review of the film was published in a foreign journal that had normally been pro-Soviet. The review was sent to the Agency.

"Don't worry. It's just a one-day story. It will pass," one optimistic Queen said to a dejected King.

10

HOTEL JOURNALISM

JUST AS POWERFUL as the Presidential Palace in Hanoi was the Caravelle Hotel in Saigon. That hotel was the center of a new journalistic technique invented by U.S. foreign correspondents.

Many of the leading U.S. foreign correspondents located in Saigon stayed there and they would meet for breakfast at 6:00 in the morning at the hotel's La Concorde Restaurant, and meet again for late afternoon drinks in the Jerome and Juliette Bar on the 8th Floor of the hotel, then go one floor up to the Champ Elysees Restaurant for dinner, and later go back to the 8th Floor Jerome and Juliette Bar for the last meeting of the night. The journalists formed a tight circle within the hotel, forming what was tantamount to a Mini-Government in Residence, looking somewhat like a president's cabinet meeting.

At the center would be the "President," who was often the

leading correspondent from ABC News, whose bureau was located at the hotel; sometimes it was a prominent journalist from another news organization, but all would be listening and contributing, sharing stories, tips, contacts, leads, and some would share advance notice of meetings and events leaked to them by their sources.

Hotel Journalism was one of the main reasons that many of the stories read, heard, and viewed back home were strikingly similar in their point of view. If some journalist was a newcomer to Saigon and checked in at the Caravelle and went to the hotel's La Concorde Restaurant or the Jerome and Juliette Bar or the Champ Elysees Restaurant at one of the times of a "cabinet meeting," he could be sure that if his political views differed from theirs and if their political nurturing was unsuccessful, there would be no more invitations to sit with them. He would soon become an outcast, and that would mean he wouldn't get the benefit of their tips and contacts. He would be eating and looking for leads—alone.

In Saigon, there was another value in joining such a group. Camaraderie had value of its own, as it always does in times and places of the unknown. There was comfort in walking the halls of the hotel at night and seeing friends who would say, "How ya doin', buddy?" rather than someone who couldn't speak English dressed in black pajamas who, for all the guest knew, could be a member of the Viet Cong. Psychological security was offered in a place where the possibility of being blown up was real. So other than courageous journalists, any originality of political thought was often given quick self-censorship.

With such a surrounding having been established, briefings

by U.S. officials became suspect. In ridicule, the U.S. press corps in Saigon used the term "the Five O'clock Follies" in describing news that came out at the daily briefings that were started by Barry Zorthian, the spokesman for the Joint U.S. Public Affairs Office. Their articles sent back home often reflected the bias of the term they used.

As is true with the Invisible Monarchy of the bureaucracy, it is the Invisible Monarchy of Hotel Journalism that worked behind the public's horizon. And just like those in the bureaucracy, there were journalists who were in zones of danger. Some were killed in performing their work. Some had no interest in the politics at the Caravelle. And it must be understood that even some who went back and forth between the Caravelle and the fields of battle found much comfort in looking forward to the support, background information, kinship, and names of sources they did not know because they were out in the fields. What is wrong is not the establishment of a hotel as a surrounding, but the way in which the structure of the hotel becomes an establishment of political thought that starts with check-in.

And that institution became a pattern that spread well beyond its inventors at the Caravelle into other then-current and oncoming major cities of international conflicts:

In Phnom Penh, Cambodia it was the Le Royal Hotel.

In Vientiane, Laos it was the Lane Xang Hotel.

In Teheran, Iran it was the Hilton.

In Beirut, Lebanon it was the Commodore.

In Managua, Nicaragua it was the Intercontinental.

In San Salvador, El Salvador it was the El Camino Real.

In Baghdad, Iraq it was the Al Rasheed Oberoi, and later, the Palestine Hotel.

Most of the American public knew nothing about Hotel Journalism since the media would certainly not tell them, except for an inadvertent hint that came out in a *Playboy* magazine interview [November, 1978] with Geraldo Rivera, regarding his reporting in Panama as the correspondent for the ABC Network during the 1977–1978 debates of President Carter's treaties on the Canal, which were the treaties giving the Canal to the Panamanian Government.

Geraldo Rivera said, "It was tremendous, if you think about it. There was ABC News, the *Times* and the *Post* having dinner together. You don't have to be a real student of the media to understand that that is a lot of power."

Earlier in the interview he said, "I am very appreciative of the power of the media. The media definitely influence events, even if people don't admit it. They're not benign observers. Let me give you an example. In my coverage of Panama, I reported every point of view, and toward the end, I was clearly in favor of the treaty. I felt that, regardless of my own personal or political feelings, or the identity I felt with the students or the Panamanian left or with the whole sense of Panamanian nationalism versus U.S. imperialism, the treaty was the best possible compromise."

He went on to tell about an incident that occurred in Panama that, if revealed to the people of the United States, could influence them against the Carter treaties. So Rivera said he downplayed it because, "That was the day I decided that I had to be very careful about what I said, because I could defeat the very thing I wanted to achieve. Later I had dinner with some people from the *New York Times* and the *Washington Post*, and we all felt the same way."

Rivera had also been on assignment in Nicaragua. "It happened in Nicaragua, too. I was talking to a group of radicals and I said, 'Listen, I'm just here to cover what is going on, but if every time I get out of my car, people are going to shoot bullets in the air, then your story is not going to get on American television. The only story that is going to get on is General Somoza's, and if that is what you want, fine, I'll go back to the hotel.'"

The interviewer then commented, "It would seem you were giving them a crash course in the proper use of the media."

The major Carter treaty, which was the *Treaty Concerning the Permanent Neutrality and Operation of the Panama Canal*, needed the votes of two-thirds of the U.S. Senate. It passed by a one-vote margin.

From the enemy's success in Southeast Asia and then beyond, it became known by enemies of the U.S. how to achieve more successes against the United States. Influencing the U.S. public *directly* was unrealistic, so it became a chief pursuit to influence members of the U.S. media, as they could serve as a bridge of credibility to the U.S. public.

The routine of Hotel Journalism gave those enemies a convenient device, which was particularly apparent in the 1980s war of El Salvador where the F.M.L.N. (Farabundo Marti National Liberation Front) Communist guerrillas were attempting to take over the government:

The only San Salvador luxury hotel left without F.M.L.N. bullet holes in the walls was the El Camino Real, where the members of the U.S. Press Corps were in residence. While Americans had been killed in the Sheraton Hotel, the El

Camino Real became a privileged sanctuary where, during some evenings, the Communist guerrillas would pick up the journalists in a van and take them to one of their mountain headquarters, give them a tour, answer their questions, serve them food and drink, and take them back to the hotel. The U.S. correspondents were not only given background on which to write, but they were flattered by the attention and closeness given them by the F.M.L.N.

At a party in San Salvador given by U.S. Ambassador Dean Hinton for some visiting Americans as well as the U.S. Press Corps in the Ambassador's residence, *Newsweek* magazine's correspondent in El Salvador said, "I advocate my position in my articles. *Newsweek* approves. I believe in advocacy journalism and *Newsweek* does take a side. What's wrong with that? Our readers have an average mentality of a seventh grader. Guiding them is no sin."

When asked what she then writes for *Newsweek*'s readers, she answered, "It depends. But I have an attraction toward the guerrillas. They're the underdogs. They're young—my age. They have their act all together. The government here doesn't."

It was a confirmation of an earlier statement made by *Washington Post* correspondent Karen DeYoung in a lecture at the Institute for Policy Studies: "Most journalists now, most Western journalists at least, are very eager to seek out guerrilla groups, leftist groups, because you assume they must be the good guys."

In 2003, Victoria "Torie" Clarke, the more than capable Assistant Secretary of Defense for Public Affairs, announced her idea, although she modestly never claimed it as her own, that changed the banding together of journalists by allowing them to be individually embedded with U.S. troops during Operation Iraqi Freedom as U.S. troops entered Iraq all the way to Baghdad. It was a rare time in post-Vietnam history when more than 500 U.S. foreign correspondents were telling their audiences, listeners, and readers back home things the public had not heard before. But the U.S. invasion, not the war, quickly ended in Baghdad, where Hotel Journalism immediately re-emerged at the Palestine Hotel.

Those who opposed the embedding of journalists with our troops often expressed the thought that "the press is forced into a form of Stockholm Syndrome, of catering to the wishes of those who have jurisdiction over their food, shelter, safety, and are responsible for their very lives." If so, then the Stockholm Syndrome may well be the reason why so many journalists cater to the enemy when they are embedded with each other practicing Hotel Journalism. There is no place of neutrality.

Back in the late 1960s and the early 1970s, while journalists stayed at the Caravelle Hotel in Saigon, other Americans were staying at hotels of captivity, among them the Hanoi Hilton [as defined in Chapter One], where torture was as common as breathing was to most Americans. A prisoner at the Hanoi Hilton was being tortured because of his refusal to sign a "confession as a criminal acting against the Vietnamese people" and his refusal to tell the names of those American officers "in charge" of other American prisoners. The torture cell was a daily ordeal. In the evenings when he was brought back to his own cell he was ordered to stand at attention for six hours. His laughing guard took great joy when the prisoner involuntarily emitted bodily functions, including vomit, and was forced to wipe it all up from the floor with his bare hands, then beaten with a rubber hose for having to take time from standing at attention. At uneven intervals, that guard put the point of his ballpoint pen into the prisoner's eyes as the prisoner tried to remain silent. He would hear screams from other torture cells, and at the sound, his own guard would laugh.

It was frequent that a tortured prisoner, when finally left in his own cell, would tap code messages on the wall to the adjoining cell, telling the prisoner in that adjoining cell that he was alright. They generally did not use Morse Code, as it was difficult to distinguish dots from dashes. Instead they used an old miner's code in which combinations of taps would represent letters of the alphabet. If any tapping was discovered by guards, there would be additional torture. Even with such a prospect, almost every night there were frequent taps of the letters G.N.G.B.U., meaning "Good Night, God Bless You." Some, trying to be light, tapped "G.N.G.B.G.C." meaning "God Bless the Gravel Crunchers."

Rear Admiral James Stockdale disfigured himself to avoid any exploitation by North Vietnamese propagandists. When they demanded information from him regarding other prisoners, he wounded himself again in a horrible way, thus proving to his captors that he would sooner be tortured than implicate other prisoners for what he was told they said or did. It was frequent for other prisoners to tap on the walls G.B.U.J.S. which stood for "God Bless You, Jim Stockdale."

Additional warnings of torture (always called "punishment" rather than torture) were made when any "U.S. Peace Activist" visited the prison camp, with threats being given to the prisoners should there be denial of the demand to meet with the visitors, or refusal to pose for photos with them. Many refused the demands.

Michael D. Benge was unique in that he was not a member of the U.S. Armed Forces but was a U.S. civilian Economic Development Officer in the central highlands of South Vietnam. During the 1968 Tet Offensive he was captured. His Viet Cong and North Vietnamese captors poisoned, then murdered a female missionary, a nurse in a leprosarium in Bam Be Thot, whom he buried in the jungle near the Cambodian border. Benge was held in captivity for the next five years, being released in Operation Homecoming. During those five years he was moved by his captors to prison camps in Cambodia, Laos, and North Vietnam, spending one year in a cage in Cambodia, 27 months in solitary confinement, and one year in a "black box." When he was asked what he would say to Jane Fonda should he visit with her in prison, he told his captors that he would tell her about the real treatment, which was far different than the treatment purported by the North Vietnamese. As a result of that reply, he spent three days on a rocky floor on his knees with outstretched arms, a steel bar placed on his open hands, and beaten with a bamboo cane every time his arms dipped.

A typical cell at Hoa Lo (the Hanoi Hilton) was semi-dark and windowless with a steel plate with some holes in it near the top of the door for air. Most of the cells were six feet by eight feet, with a stone bed for rest while shackled.

A Navy Commander was beaten daily while in a three foot by five foot windowless cell, for four months. A Lieutenant Commander was hung by his broken arm attached to a rope, then dropped by the end of the rope time after time, as the table on which he stood was kicked out from under him. A Captain was hung under his elbows from rounded hooks on his cell wall and beaten into unconsciousness with bamboo sticks. Another was locked in ankle irons while naked, forced to lie on his stomach while one guard stood on the back of his neck and jumped, and another guard beat him from shoulders to feet with a rubber hose.

There were the odors of wounds that were left without any treatment or covering. There were rats that would eat wounds while the prisoner was held in wrist and leg irons, incapable of fighting the rats. There were continual floggings to the point of vomiting blood. There were several prisoners who contracted near-insane hallucinations.

There was the storage stall in which garbage from the guards was dumped with rats and roaches rivaling the amount of garbage, becoming a room for shackled prisoners. Beyond every unimaginable device of torture, throughout the cells there was the constant odor of vomit and human waste that was left uncollected. None of this was unique but, rather, it was commonplace.

Navy Lieutenant Commander Eugene McDaniel, during a two-week period in isolation, received approximately 700 lashes with a rubber whip.

For obvious reasons, none of the individual tortures will be further detailed here beyond those summarized above.

Each prisoner in North Vietnam who did not bend to their captors had his own system of endurance. Survival was considered by the prisoners to be their victory. Some did not know that victory.

* * *

The statements of those who had been U.S. prisoners of war made little, if any, national media attention. [Ranks given below were the ranks of the prisoners while serving in Southeast Asia, including while in captivity by the North Vietnamese.]

Among those statements, Colonel James Kasler said that those prisoners meeting with delegations who came to Hanoi were handed the questions and answers, and the prisoners had to go in and perform. He said the prisoners were tortured to rehearse what should be answered and that many times the prisoners were tortured again, just to show the others what would happen to them if they failed at the conference. He added, "President Nixon brought us home with honor. God Bless those Americans who supported our President during this long ordeal."

Commander John Fellows said, "I personally hope that the people who came to Hanoi representing the dissident groups in our country can someday be brought to trial on this, or forced to answer for this. I feel that I personally stayed two extra years because of the groups that kept pressing and pressing for a split in our country."

Captain James Mulligan said, "If I had my way, I would personally like to see them tried, convicted, and sentenced for what they did to me and my friends in Hanoi. They tried to use my family against my country, and tried to deprive me of my legal rights under the Geneva Convention. And the media— why do you think we're so disturbed by the *New York Times?* While Harrison Salisbury was sitting in Hanoi, me and other guys were being tortured. And I know that he knew nothing about it. He was completely duped."

Captain Harry Jenkins said, "Probably the press is partly to blame for this—the items that were covered, that were talked about. Americans are an impetuous people. We haven't the patience."

Lieutenant Commander John McCain said, "These people, Ramsey Clark, Tom Hayden, and Jane Fonda, were on the side of the North Vietnamese. I think she only saw eight selected prisoners. I was beaten unmercifully for refusing to meet with the visitors."

Major Harold Kushner said, "I think the purposes of Fonda and Clark were to hurt the United States, to radicalize our young people, and to undermine our authority."

Major Norman McDaniel said, "I think that the division on the war, whatever amount of it existed, did in fact prolong our stay there."

Captain Jeremiah Denton said, "It hurt all of us deeply that many of our own citizens, and even some of our Senators and Congressmen back at home, were taking the enemy's side in all this. We were pretty much at a nadir in morale by 1967 and '68, but we never gave up."

Major Jon Reynolds said, "I have always maintained that the anti-war movement in the United States lengthened our stay. It was a source of strength to the North Vietnamese."

Captain J. Charles Plumb said, "I had several interrogations, called 'quizzes,' in which senior NVN officers told me that the majority of Americans were on their side, and the war would end when those 'patriotic' citizens overthrew the 'illegal gang in Washington.' To validate their argument they would pull out news articles of demonstrations against the war and quotes from the anti-war element. They seemed to confuse opposition to the war with support for the communists. Any luminary who came out against the war was suddenly their hero. I was continually amazed that these mature leaders misunderstood human dynamics. The end result was one of unintended consequences. I suspect that neither the anti-war folks nor the journalists at the Caravelle knew what damage they were doing by siding with the enemy, but I agree with my pals that their actions extended the war for at least two years."

Colonel Robinson Risner said, "I feel beyond any doubt that those people kept us in prison an extra year or two. Not just the people demonstrating, but the people who were downing or bad-mouthing our government and our policies. There is no doubt in my mind, and it was very evident to all of us, that the communist's spirit or morale went up and down along with the amount of demonstrations, protests, and anti-war movement back in the States. I could not see stopping aid to the countries I knew needed the aid. I could not see abandoning our friends and allies."

Colonel George (Bud) Day said, "I was deeply humbled by the Medal of Honor that was given to me by President Ford, but I knew that without President Nixon's conviction and courage, I would have never survived the Hanoi Hilton. It is for this reason that after the White House ceremony with President Ford, I made a special trip to see Former President Nixon in San Clemente for him to ceremonially give me the Medal of Honor. I also told him that in the Hanoi Hilton we were subjected to hearing the Jane Fonda broadcast that she gave in support of our captors, and replayed and replayed it to us in order to demoralize our spirit. Ultimately, she and her fellow Hollywood cohorts helped cause the wholesale slaughter of millions of people in Cambodia and Vietnam."

Colonel Alan Brunstrom said, "We felt that any Westerners who showed up in Hanoi were on the other side. They gave aid and comfort to the enemy, and as far as I'm concerned, they were traitors."

Jane Fonda said of the returned Prisoners of War, "They are liars and hypocrites, and history will judge them severely."

Hotel Journalism was born in Saigon, South Vietnam, where it is likely that the journalists at the Caravelle Hotel did not know what was going on up north at the Hanoi Hilton, but, at least, they later learned.

It is also safe to assume that both the prisoners and the journalists received strength from the camaraderie of their peers at their respective hotels.

Ask anyone who sent tapped messages to a friend on his cell wall at the Hanoi Hilton, or anyone who stayed at the Caravelle Hotel in Saigon and had a drink with a friend at its 8th Floor Jerome and Juliette Bar.

11

ERASING AN OLD SUPREME COURT DECISION

THERE WERE SCHOOLS of law professors at prominent U.S. east-coast universities who quickly mastered the art of erasure during the years of the Southeast Asian War.

At that time, lists of major U.S. Supreme Court decisions had often included *United States v. Curtiss-Wright Export Corporation*, dealing with the powers of the president versus the powers of the congress over the issue of foreign policy, and it had been decided in a way that knocked many political advocacies of law professors for a loop.

The reason it knocked them for a loop is because they had already accurately told their classrooms of students that in order to overturn a decision of the U.S. Supreme Court, either a forthcoming Supreme Court case would be decided in a way that overturned a previous decision or section of a decision, or an amendment to the Constitution would make a previous U.S.

Supreme Court decision void. Unless one of those procedures was enacted, a Supreme Court decision would, in a reasonable amount of time, be considered settled law.

But the U.S. Supreme Court's decision of the *United States v. Curtiss-Wright Export Corporation* was made in 1936, so surely at the time of the Southeast Asian War it had to be considered settled law. Plenty of time had passed for it to be overturned.

There were two solutions to the problem of those law professors: erase *United States v. Curtiss-Wright Export Corporation* from their syllabus or, if a student knew about it and brought it up, argue that the majority decision did not mean what it said—even though there was only one dissenting Justice: James Clark McReynolds. The majority decision was written by Associate Justice George Sutherland, supported by Chief Justice Charles E. Hughes and five other Justices, for a total of seven in the majority. (Justice Harlan Fiske Stone did not participate.)

The number of members of the congresses during the Southeast Asian War who had even heard of that Supreme Court decision was undoubtedly small, and most of that small number surely appreciated its mysterious disappearance from public awareness. [The Curtiss-Wright Export Corporation had been indicted for sending arms to Bolivia against an embargo ordered by President Franklin Delano Roosevelt. Curtiss-Wright's defense was that such an embargo could not be a decision of the President, but should be a congressional order. Curtiss-Wright lost.]

The most pertinent excerpts follow from the decision of *United States v. Curtiss-Wright Export Corporation,* in which "external realm" is the term used at times for what is now more frequently called "foreign affairs."

* * *

"In this vast external realm, with its important, complicated, delicate and manifold problems, the President alone has the power to speak or listen as a representative of the nation. He makes treaties with the advice and consent of the Senate; but he alone negotiates. Into the field of negotiation the Senate cannot intrude; and Congress itself is powerless to invade it. As [U.S. Congressman, later to become U.S. Secretary of State and Chief Justice of the U.S. Supreme Court, John] Marshall said in his great argument of March 7, 1800, in the House of Representatives, 'The President is the sole organ of the nation in its external relations, and its sole representative with foreign nations' . . . The Senate Committee on Foreign Relations at a very early day in our history [February 15, 1816] reported to the Senate, among other things, as follows:

"'The President is the constitutional representative of the United States with regard to foreign nations. He manages our concerns with foreign nations and must necessarily be most competent to determine when, how, and upon what subjects negotiation may be urged with the greatest prospect of success. For his conduct he is responsible to the Constitution. The committee consider(s) this responsibility the surest pledge for the faithful discharge of his duty. They think the interference of the Senate in the direction of foreign negotiations calculated to diminish that responsibility, and thereby to impair the best security for the national safety. The nature of transactions with foreign nations, moreover, requires caution and unity of design, and their success frequently depends on secrecy and dispatch.'

* * *

"It is important to bear in mind that we are here dealing not alone with an authority vested in the President by an exertion of legislative power, but with such an authority plus the very delicate, plenary and exclusive power of the President as the sole organ of the federal government in the field of international relations—a power which does not require as a basis for its exercise an act of Congress, but which, of course, like every other governmental power, must be exercised in subordination to the applicable provisions of the Constitution. It is quite apparent that if, in the maintenance of our international relations, embarrassment—perhaps serious embarrassment—is to be avoided and success for our aims achieved, congressional legislation which is to be made effective through negotiation and inquiry within the international field must often accord to the President a degree of discretion and freedom from statutory restriction which would not be admissible were domestic affairs alone involved. Moreover, he, not Congress, has the better opportunity of knowing the conditions which prevail in foreign countries, and especially is this true in time of war. He has his confidential sources of information. He has his agents in the form of diplomatic, consular and other officials. Secrecy in respect of information gathered by them may be highly necessary, and the premature disclosure of it productive of harmful results. Indeed, so clearly is this true that the First President refused to accede to a request to lay before the House of Representatives the instructions, correspondence and documents relating to the negotiation of the Jay Treaty—a refusal the wisdom of which was recognized by the House itself and has never since been doubted . . .

*   *   *

"When the President is to be authorized by legislation to act in respect of a matter intended to affect a situation in foreign territory, the legislator properly bears in mind the important consideration that the form of the President's action—or, indeed, whether he shall act at all—may well depend, among other things, upon the nature of the confidential information which he has or may thereafter receive, or upon the effect which his action may have upon our foreign relations. This consideration, in connection with what we have already said on the subject, discloses the unwisdom of requiring Congress in this field of governmental power to lay down narrowly definite standards by which the President is to be governed."

Five Presidents later, during the 1973 debate in the Congress over the War Powers Resolution, transferring major executive authority in foreign affairs to the Congress, a prominent Senator was stopped as he walked down a hallway in the Russell Senate Office Building.

"Pardon me, Senator. Am I correct in assuming you are planning to vote for the War Powers Resolution?"

"Yes, sir! You betcha! You can count on it!"

"Senator, I know you must have studied the Supreme Court decision of *United States v. Curtiss-Wright Export Corporation.* Doesn't that preclude voting for the War Powers Act? It seems like there's a conflict there."

"Curtiss who?"

"Curtiss-Wright. 1936. Executive versus the Legislature in foreign affairs."

"You betcha!"

"You mean there *is* a conflict?"

"Not at all. Not at all."

"Senator, you might re-read it because I know how many cases there are to remember and sometimes—"

"I'll do that. That's something I had down to do somewhere. The old Curtiss case. I'm glad you reminded me."

"Curtiss-Wright."

"That's the whole name. That's what it was. I'll have my staff study that. I'll study that. The staff will dig it up for me."

"Will you get back to me after you've done that, Senator?"

"Of course. Of course. You betcha. I'll get back to you on that."

At this writing, the conversation with the Senator took place 35 years ago. He still hasn't got back on that.

Maybe tomorrow.

One of the provisions of the War Powers Resolution established that the President in every possible instance should consult with Congress before introducing United States Armed Forces into hostilities, or into situations where imminent involvement in hostilities was clearly indicated by the circumstances, and after every such introduction should consult regularly with the Congress until United States Armed Forces would no longer be engaged.

Unfortunately, it didn't stop there: If, within 48 hours after consultation with the Congress, there would be agreement to go ahead and station the troops, the President would have to withdraw them within 60 days unless the Congress extended the 60-day period. And it stated that the President would be able to extend the time an additional 30 days, but only if he would certify in writing that those 30 days would be necessary to protect U.S. forces during their withdrawal.

It got worse. Not only would the President have to get the troops out of imminent hostilities by action of the Congress— but by its *inaction:* If the Congress decides to do *nothing,* our troops would have to leave an area of imminent hostilities in 60 to 90 days. Even during that 60 to 90 day period, the Resolution stated that if the Congress should want an *immediate* withdrawal of U.S. forces, they need only pass a concurrent resolution to that effect which would *not* be subject to a Presidential veto.

The War Powers Resolution became a bill that passed the Congress. But this bill, like all bills before it, was sent to the White House for the President's signature or his veto. President Nixon vetoed it, calling the bill "both unconstitutional and dangerous to the best interests of the United States." He said, "If this resolution had been in operation, America's effective response to a variety of challenges in recent years would have been vastly complicated or even made impossible. We may well have been unable to respond in the way we did during the Berlin crisis of 1961, the Cuban missile crisis of 1962, the Congo rescue operation in 1964, and the Jordanian crisis of 1970, to mention just a few examples. In addition, our recent actions to bring about a peaceful settlement of the hostilities in the Middle East [our response in the Yom Kippur War] would have been seriously impaired if this resolution had been in force."

The 93rd Congress overrode the President's veto, and the War Powers Resolution that had become a bill now became the War Powers Act, and became a weight on the shoulder of Presidents since that time.

Since it has become law, the very *threat* of Congress invoking the Act has brought about casualties.

It was discovered by the Cable News Network in February 1982 that a U.S. soldier in El Salvador, Lt. Colonel Harry Melander, was carrying an automatic rifle while he was helping Salvadoran officers replace a bridge that had been destroyed by guerrillas. Orders then came from Washington for Melander to be taken out of El Salvador, and he was reprimanded for having that loaded rifle with him while he helped replace the bridge in dangerous territory; the expulsion and the reprimand were consistent with the terms of the War Powers Act. The loaded rifle indicated "imminent hostilities."

A truck came smashing into U.S. Marine Headquarters in Beirut with a cargo of explosives on October 23, 1983, destined to kill 241 U.S. Armed Forces. It rammed through a barbed wire fence and passed through two sentry posts. At both sentry posts, the Marines on duty were armed with unloaded weapons, and the Marine guards stated that the truck was going too fast for them to load the bullet clips into their automatic rifles and then fire at the truck. They didn't have bullet clips already fastened to their rifles because they were obeying orders that were consistent with the terms of the War Powers Act. Clips would indicate "imminent hostilities."

When our ships at sea fired at Syrian-held positions that were blasting Beirut, Lebanon, on February 7, 1984, our commanders were ordered to stop, consistent with the terms of the War Powers Act. Syrian President Hafez al-Assad then knew his victory was assured. Although the U.S. Congress had extended the President's deadline to 18 months under the War Powers Act, there was an announced deadline. President Assad could wait for that deadline to come while the Reagan Administration would be unable to fire on Assad's forces or his allies unless it was a direct act of self-protection. It was not President Assad that stopped the United States when we bombarded Syrian-held positions; it was the threat of congressional abridgment of the 18-month timetable. The Administration backed off.

If our military should act beyond self-defense, suggesting that U.S. forces are in an area of imminent hostility without a declaration of war, then the President of the United States is in jeopardy of being in violation of the War Powers Act. (Throughout U.S. history, there have only been five declarations of war, while our Armed Forces have been sent on 239 foreign engagements.) If obeyed, the War Powers Act is nothing less than an announcement to the world that the President's word can be overridden by a published timetable that assures our departure from the scene. Even if the War Powers Act is not invoked, an adversary knows that by killing Americans, some members of the Congress may rush to put the Act into effect. Out-waiting the United States can then become a winning procedure anywhere in the world in which our forces are engaged.

Not one President [1973–2008] since it became law has believed it to be constitutional. [Nixon, Ford, Carter, Reagan, Bush (41), Clinton, Bush (43).] None of them wanted to give it credibility, and at the same time none wanted to blatantly act against it, so they took care not to state that they were acting "in *compliance* with" or acting "*under* its terms," but rather that they were simply acting "*consistent* with its terms" or "*took note of.*" If their military action ordered was short enough, their report to the Congress came after the completion of the intervention.

President Reagan said, "I would like to emphasize my view that the imposition of such authority and inflexible deadlines creates unwise limitations on Presidential authority to deploy U.S. forces in the interests of U.S. national security. For example, such deadlines can undermine foreign policy judgments, adversely affect our ability to deploy U.S. Armed Forces in support of those judgments, and encourage hostile elements to maximize U.S. casualties in connection with such deployments."

In a court case ten years after the passage of the War Powers Act, but separate and apart from that Act, the Supreme Court judged [on June 23, 1983] a "legislative veto" to be unconstitutional as a breach of the separation of powers. [*Immigration and Naturalization Service v. Chadha.*] Since a legislative veto was an integral part of the War Powers Act, it seemed that it would likely go silently away, but it didn't.

It came up from one administration to another, most noteworthy being the attempt by 110 members of the 100th Congress bringing President Reagan's 1987 naval operations in the Persian Gulf to the courts. But the Federal Court District Judge tossed it out, saying it was a political question and the courts shouldn't be called to resolve such issues. That still wasn't the end of it. President Clinton sent troops to Haiti [1994] and Bosnia [1995], both of which were challenged by some members of the Congress. The challenges never went anywhere. Then 31 bipartisan members of the 106th Congress tried to invoke the War Powers Act as reason to deny President Clinton the right to use military intervention in Kosovo [1999], and they brought the case through the lower courts. They lost the case, and ultimately the losing members of the Congress brought it to the Supreme Court, where the case was refused to be heard [2000]. Traditionally, with little exception in only the rarest of urgent cases, the Supreme Court avoids making political decisions in disputes between the other two branches of government.

After the failure of the congressional attempt regarding Kosovo, the invocation of the War Powers Act has become less and less of a threat as more and more members of forthcoming congresses recognized that a legislative veto is unconstitutional, and those who didn't recognize that at least knew that if those attempting to invoke the War Powers Act had to go all the way to the Supreme Court, it was unlikely to be considered. Most important of all, more members of the Congress knew that if the Supreme Court *did* agree to consider their case, the Court would be most unlikely to decide in favor of the Congress since, in order to do that, the Court would be forced to override the long-standing *United States v. Curtiss-Wright Export Corporation* Supreme Court decision that confirmed the authority of the President in issues of foreign affairs.

That does not, however, change the fact that the War Powers Act is still on the books and can come back to haunt a president in the future. Despite the fact that over seven decades have passed (at this writing) since the U.S. Supreme Court's decision of *United States v. Curtiss-Wright Export Corporation*, there have been some members of every congress since the 1970s who have been convinced they are in a legislative body of 535 Commanders in Chief, although none of them were elected to fill that office.

That illusion is likely to last a while longer.

12

FROM VIETNAM TO 9-11:

Finding and Connecting the Dots

FOR DECADES, MANY of those who were around at the time of the Southeast Asian War did not want to live in the past but to get on with the present and the future; a totally understandable position. But like most truths that have been allowed to be substituted with deception, the accepted illusion of the past became a false premise for decisions yet to be made.

Every military conflict in which the United States has been engaged since the 1975 surrenders has been compared with Vietnam.

The phrase "another Vietnam" became so commonly used in opposition to current or potential U.S. military engagements that, in time, the two words seemed to be glued to become one word: "anothervietnam."

* * *

The distorted history of what led to the defeat of South Vietnam, Cambodia, and Laos led to long-range consequences well beyond Southeast Asia: After 9-11 we soon became armed with reports of governmental committees that purported to identify how our intelligence failed us and enabled 9-11 to take place. Among the reports were the most prominent 858-page Joint House and Senate Congressional Report and the 567-page 9-11 Commission Report. All told, the reports gave some 162 conclusions and recommendations.

Many of those who authored the reports attempted to "connect the dots" created during the years of the Clinton and G. W. Bush Administrations. Those reports made one unforgivable error: they deleted the most significant dots, the ones that were created before those two Administrations began, with some of the authors of the reports having been the creators of those dots.

The first dot should have been recorded as the steps taken by the 93rd Congress to remove the foreign policy authority of the President, transferring it to the Congress through continually attaching riders to funding bills to "end the war" in Vietnam, culminating in the War Powers Act. Another dot was the reaction to Watergate that within months of President Nixon's resignation brought about the tremendous majority achieved by the incoming 94th Congress [Chapter Two]. Even before its final betrayal of the Paris Peace Accords, there was another dot that would lead to 9-11.

Almost as soon as the 94th Congress convened, it assembled a number of congressional committees to investigate U.S. intelligence agencies: the Rockefeller Commission, the House Select Intelligence Committee [known as the Nedzi Committee and became the Pike Committee], and, most prominent, the Senate-Select Committee to Study Government Operations with Respect to Intelligence Activities, with Senator Frank Church of Idaho as its chairman. That committee became known as the Senate-Select Committee on Intelligence, or the Church Committee.

Prior to then, the Central Intelligence Agency was recognized worldwide as one of the three great international intelligence agencies of the free world, along with MI–6 of Great Britain and Mossad of Israel. If someone wanted to phone the C.I.A., they would not find it listed in any phonebook. If someone wanted to see it, they would find no identifying sign along the George Washington Parkway for the correct turn-off to the facility. Those who worked in senior positions of other departments, agencies, and bureaus in Washington, D. C. were not to refer to it by name but only as "our friends across the river," to remind the speaker that before saying anything that might be classified, he or she should first be sure of the security clearances and need-to-know of those in attendance. The budget of the C.I.A. was held so secret that only limited members of the Congress knew its total. It operated largely on what was called a "black budget," which was supplied by the departments, agencies, and bureaus of government contributing a designated amount of their own budget to the C.I.A. but identified with false headings, without its officers knowing what other departments, agencies, and bureaus were contributing.

Much of the secretiveness was condemned by the 94th Congress' Senate-Select Committee on Intelligence. In addition, it recommended that C.I.A. agents no longer deal with "dirty" foreign groups that our intelligence had always deemed necessary to infiltrate, nor should one U.S. intelligence agency connect with other U.S. agencies on individual cases that could blur the distinction between foreign and domestic spying. The committee also composed a list of those activities from which our intelligence agencies should disengage. Worst of all, on February the 27th of 1975, Senator Church announced that the secrecy oath signed by all C.I.A. employees would be waived, and C.I.A. agents should testify to his committee about those things they had previously sworn to hold secret. C.I.A. Director William Colby agreed.

Some of the finest agents remained silent. After all, they couldn't or wouldn't break their word given in a previously made oath. Other conscientious agents justifiably took early retirement rather than testify. Some simply resigned, while some agents *did* testify. Revelations turned into an outpouring. A torrent of information was spread around the world, aided by dissidents and defectors who had once been with the Agency.

In one country after another, previously held secrets were printed in anti-U.S. magazines. There were revelations printed in *Liberacion* magazine and *Anti* magazine and *Counterspy* magazine. A magazine called *Covert Action Information Bulletin* exposed over 1,000 names of C.I.A. agents and foreign informants. Richard Welch, U.S. Station Chief in Athens (our C.I.A. agent there) was assassinated by three masked gunmen on December the 23rd of that year on his way home from a Christmas party after his name was revealed. He was 46 years old. President Ford neither confirmed nor denied that Richard Welch was part of the C.I.A., but there was little public doubt that he was with the C.I.A., as President Ford allowed the burial of Richard Welch at Arlington National Cemetery, although Richard Welch would not have been eligible for burial at Arlington since he did not serve in the U.S. Armed Forces or qualify under any ordinary exceptions to that requirement.

It soon became near-impossible to keep or find citizens of foreign countries to help the C.I.A. Foreign informants declined by 93%. Those who dropped their affiliation felt that if they continued to serve the C.I.A., the jeopardy under which they served would be too much of a risk to their families and to themselves. They faced the possibility of disclosures from the very nation to whom they had given so much. Ours.

Howard Simons, the Managing Editor of the *Washington Post*, had said in reference to the C.I.A. Director: "It's his job to keep secrets. That's his job. My job is to find them." Dan Rather of CBS had said, "My job is to publish and be damned."

During the April 10th, 1975 speech President Ford gave to a Joint Session of the 94th Congress regarding funds for Vietnam and Cambodia [excerpts in Chapter Two], President Ford also said, "Let me speak quite frankly to some in this Chamber and perhaps to some not in this Chamber. The Central Intelligence Agency has been of maximum importance to Presidents before me. The Central Intelligence Agency has been of maximum importance to me. The Central Intelligence Agency and its associated intelligence organizations could be of maximum importance to some of you in this audience who might be President at some later date. I think it would be catastrophic for the Congress or anyone else to destroy the usefulness by dismantling, in effect, our intelligence systems, upon which we rest so heavily."

But, just like his plea for aid to South Vietnam and Cambodia, his plea on retaining our intelligence capabilities were disregarded by the 94th Congress. Those intelligence capabilities were ruined, and their ruination caused one intelligence failure after another.

Even after 9-11 we had to employ a coalition of intelligence from other nations who did not have a reputation of public exposure. The preceding generation of foreign C.I.A. informants advised their sons and daughters and young friends to work only for those governments that were known to hold confidence, and not to work for any government that was known to have betrayed confidence.

Betrayal in national security and foreign policy became common. When Jimmy Carter became President, he took his cue from the State Department and from the success of recent Congresses. His Administration betrayed one foreign friend of the United States after another: President Romero of El Salvador, resulting in a war with the Marxist Guerrillas of the F.M.L.N.; President Somoza of Nicaragua, resulting in the success of the Sandinistas takeover; transferring diplomatic relations from Taiwan to the People's Republic of China; and betraying the Shah of Iran, an act that ushered in the Ayatollah Khomeini. It was well known within our government that the Ayatollah Khomeini was waiting in Paris for the Shah to leave. Khomeini's wait was over on February 1, 1979. He quickly took the reins of Iran's government. The Carter White House and the State Department were in glee, as though Khomeini would be a savior. Our U.S. Ambassador to the United Nations, Andrew Young, stated,

"Khomeini will be somewhat of a Saint when we get over the panic." Iran then became the first Fundamentalist Revolutionary Islamist Government, with terrorism as its backbone. That provided others in neighboring countries to raise a facsimile of his baton. There were a number of Arab leaders who did not want a Persian to be the idol of Islam. *They* wanted that title.

The two ingredients of February 27, 1975 and February 1, 1979 were stirred together: the death of our major intelligence agency and the birth of an Islamist fundamentalist revolutionary terrorist government.

There is an old and wise Arab expression: "It is written." And it was written that it was only a matter of time before the steaming cauldron of those two ingredients would result in tragedies for the peoples of the United States and peoples of other nations around the world.

And so the world was destined to change for the worse.

All of the above events were connected. The dots that led to 9-11 didn't require commissions. It only required a memory.

What would have happened if our intelligence capabilities had been retained *without* the 94th Congress being so immersed in the Anti-Vietnam aura? Imagine the C.I.A. had retained its previously held abilities and mission. Imagine, then, that the following scenario occurred:

Assume that the director of the C.I.A., George Tenet, came into the Oval Office in July of 2001 and said, "Mr. President, I have very tough news. Based on information from unassailable foreign informants, there will be a massive attack on the United

States some two months or so from today. It is being planned by Al Qaeda, sheltered by the Taliban Government of Afghanistan. Our operatives have been associating with them. The attack will be directly committed by 19 Islamic fundamentalists, 15 of them here from Saudi Arabia. Our friends at the Bureau have been conducting surveillance on all 19. We know where they are. And I must stress that our people and the foreign informants who confirmed this information are beyond reproach. Totally reliable. We do not know where the attack will take place on our country or how, but the plan is for the attack to be like nothing we've known before, and it is planned to cause a tremendous catastrophe to the United States."

After some questioning and conversation, Director Tenet walks from the Oval Office, leaving the President alone. And the President thinks. And paces. And thinks. And paces. And thinks.

Based on the information he has been given, the President orders preemptive action, including the bombing and invasion of Afghanistan to bring about a regime change from Mullah Muhammad Omar of the Taliban Government.

The President is successful, and he reduces Al Qaeda to hiding in caves. Moreover, within the United States, the President quickly orders the immediate arrest of the 19 men who were scheduled to perform the attack on the United States, and they are imprisoned in Guantanamo Bay Naval Base.

Then comes September the 11th—and nothing happens. It is a normal Tuesday in the United States. Baseball games, preparations continue for the Emmy Awards, ESPN has an interview with tennis champion Venus Williams, the nightly news has a segment on a flurry of shark attacks, Washington D.C. is talking about the hearings on the appointment of John Negroponte as our Ambassador to the UN. An ordinary September day. And most important of all, away from the news, those who walked into New York City's twin towers of the World Trade Center in the morning walk out of those buildings in the evening. And they go to their homes. And it's a routine day at the Pentagon, and a routine day in Somerset County, Pennsylvania.

Now imagine that the mindset of the Vietnam years was suddenly restored. Even if all the above had occurred, with the Anti-Vietnam mindset suddenly reinstated, the President would be condemned. "After all," it would have been said, "we suddenly bombed and overthrew the government of a foreign country, even though that government never did anything against the United States, and they had no weapons of mass destruction or even any weapons beyond the most primitive. What could they have possibly used against us? And we imprisoned 19 people. We sent them to Guantanamo without any evidence they did anything!"

Although the President's preemptive actions would have saved the lives of some 3,000 people and the grief of countless more, his Presidency would probably have been over. Who would have believed that he acted wisely, particularly if he didn't give the sources of intelligence, so as not to jeopardize their safety?

But, of course, none of that happened.

* * *

In the first two weeks after 9-11 it was apparent to the nation that preemptive action would be necessary to avoid such a future catastrophe. That didn't last long. Move the calendar forward to 2003, not to another hypothetical scenario, but a real one: Many who served on the commissions that later concluded that President George W. Bush did not "connect the dots" that led to 9-11, without even a blink of hesitancy, accused the President of taking preemptive action against Iraq, which for sure was a threat in which he *did* connect the dots: the dots of Saddam Hussein's history of terrorism, rape rooms for women, throwing male prisoners from the top of buildings, his hatred for the United States, the planned but thwarted bombing of Radio Free Europe and Radio Liberty facilities in the Czech Republic, his invasion of Kuwait, our monitoring of no-fly zones for the ten years following our liberation of Kuwait while Saddam Hussein's government tried to shoot our monitoring planes down, the intended assassination of President Bush (41) in Kuwait, his financial rewards to families of Arab-Palestinian suicide bombers, and his use of chemical weapons on Shias and Kurds. These were all dots, including warnings of weapons of mass destruction given to the President by our C.I.A.; by the S.I.S. [MI–6], the British Secret Intelligence Service; by the D.G.S.E., the French Directorate-General for External Security; by the B.N.D., the German's Intelligence Bundesnachrichtendienst; by President Hosni Mubarak of Egypt; by King Abdullah II of Jordan; and even by President Vladimir Putin of Russia. Could any responsible President of the United States have ignored such warnings? Such dots?

With the constant use of the term "anothervietnam," and "we are in anothervietnam quagmire" an everyday part of congressional dialogue, the 110th Congress tried to withdraw U.S. Armed Forces from Iraq. In July of 2007, Senators Carl Levin and Jack Reed introduced an amendment [a rider] to the National Defense Authorization Bill for Fiscal Year 2008, calling for the withdrawal of U.S. Armed Forces from Iraq, with the withdrawal beginning in 120 days after enactment, and for the process to be completed by April 30, 2008. Perhaps it was coincidental, but that date for completion would have been the 33rd Anniversary of the surrender of South Vietnam.

It was as though the 110th Congress was trying to emulate the same fate that was brought about by the 94th Congress, this time in the Mideast rather than in Southeast Asia. Although the amendment calling for the withdrawal from Iraq received the majority of Senate votes [52-47] it did not receive the 60 votes necessary to invoke cloture that would end a filibuster, and so the amendment failed to be part of the National Defense Authorization Act.

The great long-term harm that has been done by the dissent over our preemptive action in Iraq is that preemptive action is now known to be a tremendous *domestic* risk for a president. It is entirely possible that, knowing the dissenting reactions of many regarding Iraq, a president may not do what must be done for our survival as a nation: take preemptive actions— likely against the government of Iran or North Korea or Syria or Somalia or Yemen or some other menacing state, or Hezbollah or Hamas. Some president may wait until it's too late rather than suffer *domestic* political consequences.

Because of congressional actions taken in the mid-1970s, the nation today faces risks to our survival, and risks to the very survival of civilization as we know it.

Voluntary amnesia is a crime against history. When there was a Soviet Union, its government was a master of voluntary amnesia. In the early 1960s the Soviet government decided Joseph

Stalin had never existed. Beyond the government's justifiable removal of memorials to him, there was the *un*justifiable quick printing of new history textbooks vacant of his name and vacant of the horrors he committed. In the early and mid-1960s the Soviet Union ignored the space accomplishments of the United States and, by ignoring them, turned them into non-events. In the early 1970s Aleksandr Solzhenitsyn's *The Gulag Archipelago*, that recorded the atrocities endured by massive numbers of political prisoners in the Soviet Union, was a non-book. Within their system, historical revisions, non-events, and non-books ran invisibly rampant.

It can't happen here, we all thought. But it did. Like Stalin, space capsules, and Solzhenitsyn, erasures have been made in our recorded history of the Southeast Asian War and the fall of South Vietnam, Cambodia, and Laos. And by the erasures, old times there have been forgotten.

The consequences of such voluntary amnesia is that not only current but *future* educators, major media, protesters, and congresses will create yet another circle of influence, building new times here on a foundation of fantasy destined to crumble beneath our feet.

INDEX